INHALT

So viele Zeichen im Workbook – was bedeuten sie?

Die Ampel – Wie schwer fällt dir eine Übung?
In der Ampel kannst du markieren, wie schwer dir eine (Teil-)Übung gefallen ist: rot = schwer, gelb = mittel, grün = leicht.

Leere und volle Kreise – jeder so gut er kann
Leichtere Aufgaben sind mit einem leeren Kreis markiert und schwierigere mit einem vollen. Die Übungen ohne spezielle Markierungen sind auf einem Niveau, das alle Schülerinnen und Schüler lösen können.

Kopfhörer und Quick Codes – Hören von der CD, Üben und Spielen auf dem Computer
3
Für diese beiden Angebote brauchst du noch ein anderes Medium als nur dein Workbook: Die Zahl unter dem Kopfhörer nennt dir die Track-Nummer, unter der du den entsprechenden Hörtext auf der Audio-CD findest.
5518
Das e-Workbook bietet dir viele zusätzliche, interaktive Übungen an. Der Quick Code im Workbook verweist auf die passende Aufgabe im e-Workbook.

Stift und Partnerarbeit – wie du diese Übungen bearbeiten sollst
Für Aufgaben, neben denen ein Stift abgebildet ist, schreibst du deine Antwort auf ein anderes Blatt Papier. Die beiden Köpfe beziehen sich auf Übungen, die du mit einer Partnerin / mit einem Partner bearbeiten kannst.

Unit 1 Together again

1 Pictures of summer

Look at the picture. Then complete the words in the sentences below.

In the picture on the left there's a lake in front of some mountains.

Here a family is having a barbecue.

In the picture on the right I can see the sea and a sandy beach.

There's a harbour with boats and some people are on a ferry.

And the weather? On the right it's hot and sunny.

But on the l eft it's cold and rainy.

► SB p. 9

020

2 In the holidays

a) Complete the sentences.

was • wasn't • were • weren't

1 Adam and his dad were (✓) in London and the weather wasn't (✗) nice.

2 Adam watched a football game when he was (✓) in Wembley but it wasn't (✗) a good game.

3 Adam's friends weren't (✗) with him. Berry wasn't (✗) in England! She was (✓) in the USA.

b) Now write three sentences about your holidays.

Exercise 2 on page 9 of the student's book can help you.

1 ...

2 ...

3 ...

► SB p. 9

3 Back at school

a) Listen and complete the sentences. 2

Ellie, Luca and Adam *went* back to Eggy in September. They talked *about* Ellie's holiday with her dad in Spain. Ellie said that Spain was *great* and Luca said he *stayed* in Plymouth. Adam tried to be *funny*, but Ellie was fed up. *Poor* Ellie! She was very unhappy because she *missed* Berry. But Luca said the good thing was that Berry liked *the US* – she said so in her blog.

b) Listen again. ~~Cross out~~ the mistake in these sentences and write the correct word. 3

1 In July, Amy went to the ~~sea~~ with her parents and grandparents. *mountains*

2 The family were very happy because most days, the weather was very ~~warm~~. *sunny*

3 Amy wants to go back to the same place next ~~holidays~~, but her dad wants to go to Turkey.

summer

0303

► SB p. 10

4 Berry in the US

Write sentences for the pictures. Pick the right form of the verbs in red!

1

Berry – go – the US – July. / really excited.

Berry *went to the US in July.*

She *was really excited*.

2

read – friends' texts. / happy.

She read her friends' text. She was happy.

3

one day – help – aunt – garden. / It – fun.

One day she helped her aunt in the garden. It was fun.

4

visit – aunt's friends – and meet – lots of friendly people.

She visited her aunt's friends and met lots of friendly people.

0304

► SB p. 10

5 Feelings

Write three sentences about feelings.

Example: *I feel excited and quite nervous when I join a new club.*

Ideas:
happy/unhappy/excited/nervous/lonely/bored/fed up/sad
when ... I'm alone / I miss my friends / it's my birthday / my friends text me

1 I feel ... ______

2 ... ______

3 ... ______

▸ SB p. 11

6 Mia had another bad day

a) Use arrows → and make sentences about Mia's day.
Then say the sentences with your partner.

You can colour each sentence.

Wednesday last	week was a	I was fed	up at the end	of the day!
my bus was	bad day. First	wasn't happy.	the teacher	homework, so
50 minutes	break, and I	was alone.	After break	have my
late. The	that there was	hard. After	we had	boring. I didn't
second lesson	was science and	it was really	geography, but	it was really

040

b) Write about a really bad or really good day at school. You can find some ideas in a).

▸ SB p. 11

7 What they do at at Eggy school clubs

a) Write the missing words.

1 At the adventure club – last year they learned about *rock* *climbing*. They went on a *three-day* *trip* to Cornwall.

2 At the drama club – they did a *Christmas* *pantomime*.

3 At the science club – they do lots of great *experiments*.

b) What do you think they do at these clubs?

1 At the volleyball club – *(they play volleyball)*.

2 At the book club – I think they *(read and talk about books)*.

3 At the French club – I think they *(speak French / learn about France)*.

040

▸ SB p. 12

8 John's holiday in St Andrews

Write sentences for Ellie's friend John. Put the verbs in the simple past.

1 I started my holiday on 5th July.
start – holiday – 5th July

2 My uncle in St Andrews invited me so I stayed with him.
uncle in St Andrews – invite – me – so I – stay – him

3 We visited lots of cool places in St Andrews.
visit – lots of – cool places – St Andrews

4 I really liked the harbour.
really like – harbour

5 In the evening we cooked and washed up together.
evening – cook – wash up – together

6 It wasn't boring. We talked and we laughed a lot.
talk – laugh – a lot

0508

▸ SB p. 15

9 Verb check

a) Write the verbs in the simple past.

These are verbs you have to learn!

1 go 2 meet 3 feel 4 have 5 be
6 make 7 find 8 get 9 drive 10 write

1				t
	w		l	
2	m	e	t	
	f		n	
3				t

4				e
	h		d	
5	w	a	s	
	m		d	
6				

			10			
	7		w		e	
		f	r	v		
	8	g	o	t		
		r	t	u		
	d		e		n	
9						d

b) Write funny sentences with TWO verbs from 9 a) in them.

Example: I drove into town and found a crocodile.

1 ... .

2 ... .

0509

Compare with your partner. Who wrote the funniest sentences?

▸ SB p. 15

10 John talks about the weekend

Write the verbs in the simple past.

Last weekend my family and I *(drive)* drove to the seaside. We *(meet)* met some friends, so they *(join)* joined us and we all *(go)* went swimming in the sea. The water *(be)* was really cold! We *(see)* saw lots of boats on the sea – they *(be)* were quite big. My dad *(find)* found a football, so we *(play)* played football on the beach.

My little sister Annie *(make)* made lots of sandcastles and she *(look)* looked at crabs in the water. Then she *(want)* wanted an ice-cream, so we all *(have)* had one. Yummy!

Annie likes sandcastles.

► SB p. 15

11 Berry's first day at school

Write the verbs in the simple past.

1. *(~~sleep~~)* Berry didn't sleep long the night before her first day at school.
2. *(~~have~~)* She was nervous, so she didn't have breakfast.
3. *(~~need~~)* She didn't need a uniform for school.
4. *(~~use~~)* She didn't use the bus on her first day. She drove with her mum.
5. *(~~know~~)* She didn't know the students in her class.
6. *(~~always understand~~)* They were friendly and talked to her, but Berry didn't always understand them!

0611

► SB p. 16

12 NOW YOU

a) Write what you didn't do yesterday!
Write three sentences and use these verbs.

Examples: I didn't come to school with my friends.
I didn't come to school by helicopter!

1 ~~come to school~~ ______________________

2 ~~have lunch~~ ______________________

3 ~~go~~ ______________________

b) Write three more sentences – *your* ideas!

► SB p. 16

13 No, that's wrong!

The sentences about the first day back at Eggy are wrong. Write what is wrong and write the correct information.

Look at page 10 in your book!

1 "School started at 8 o'clock."

No! *School didn't start at 8 o'clock! It started at* *8.45*.

2 "Ellie had a bad summer."

No! Ellie didn't *have a bad summer*! She *had a good/great summer*.

3 "Ellie went to Spain with her mum."

No! Ellie *didn't go to Spain with her mum*! She *went there with her dad*.

4 "Luca got up early every day."

No! Luca *didn't get up early every day*! He *stayed in bed / got up late*.

5 "Ellie felt happy to be back at school."

No! Ellie *didn't feel happy*! She *felt unhappy / she missed Berry*.

0713

6 "Luca phoned Berry yesterday."

No! He *didn't phone her*! He *read her blog*.

► SB p. 16

14 Excuses[1]

Write three good excuses. Use the simple past.

1

Sorry! I didn't phone you because ... ____

2

Sorry, Sir! I didn't ... ____ because ... ____

3

Sorry, mum! I didn't ... ____ because ... ____

► SB p. 16

[1] excuse (n.) *Ausrede*

15 What happened in the story?

Read the three summaries of the story. Which summary is right? A ☐ B ☑ C ☐

(A) At first, Ellie was unhappy because Adam and Luca were unfriendly to her. Then she found a new friend: Mia, and she didn't need Adam and Luca. Ellie felt good again.

(B) At first, Ellie was jealous because Adam and Luca were very friendly to Mia. But when she understood that Mia was unhappy and needed friends, she felt terrible. So she was nice to Mia and she felt better, too.

(C) At first, Ellie felt lonely because Berry was in America. She felt terrible. But then Mia came and sat next to her in the canteen at lunchtime, and she talked to Ellie about her family. So Ellie felt happy again.

► SB p. 19

16 Why? Because …

Complete the sentences.

You can find ideas for answers in the story on pages 17 and 18 in your book.

1 Ellie was unhappy on Monday morning

… because *she missed Berry* and because *Luca and Adam were with Mia*.

2 Ellie was surprised on Monday afternoon

… because *she waited for Adam and Luca and they didn't come*.

3 Adam and Luca weren't with Mia in the canteen on Tuesday lunchtime

… because *they were at the football club*.

4 Mia was "just like Berry"

… because *Berry and Mia were new at school / didn't have friends / etc*.

5 Mia was sad on Tuesday lunchtime

… because *she missed her friends / was lonely / Mum died / etc*.

6 Mia was happy at the end of the story

… because *Ellie was nice to her / she had friends at Eggy / etc*.

► SB p. 19

0816

17 Words in the story

Find the simple past forms of these verbs in the story. Write them in the crossword.

Across ➜
3 understand
7 answer
10 eat
11 think

Down ⬇
1 meet
2 get
4 die
5 come
6 feel
8 see
9 sit

			1 M				2 G							
3 U	N	D	E	R	S	T	O	O	4 D					
			T				T		I					
		5 C				6 F			E					
		7 A	N	8 S	W	E	R	E	D			9 S		
		M		A		L						10 A	T	E
		E		W		11 T	H	O	U	G	H	T		

► SB p. 19

18 WORDS Word fields

a) Write words in these word fields. How many can you write?

places / (in) town	people / family	school clubs	food
zoo	mother	homework club	cheese
cafe	stepbrother	adventure club	soup
cinema	father	karate club	chips
market	grandma	canoe club	cream
restaurant	grandpa	drama club	apple
stadium	sister	puppet club	scone
swimming pool	stepdad	music club	sandwich

0918

► SB p. 20

b) Write good names for the word fields. Are your names the same as your partner's?

19 WORDS Learning phrases

a) What goes together? Complete the phrases.

How can you remember words? Here's another idea: Learn some words in useful phrases.
For example: like ► I'd like to see you again.

1 welcome ► Welcome to the club!

2 sit ► Come and sit next to (me).

3 wait ► We can wait for the other (students).

4 think ► Can you think of some questions?

5 nice ► It's nice to be (together).

6 why ► That's why we came here.

... we came here.
... for the other ...
... to be ...
... to the club!
... next to ...
... of some questions?

b) Write four more sentences/phrases with these words.

1 beautiful ► ...

2 long ► ...

3 clothes ► ...

4 fun ► ...

► SB p. 20

20 WRITING Linking words. John's weekend

a) Choose the right word and complete the sentence.

1 *(because / but)* On Friday I phoned Ellie because I was in Plymouth for the weekend.

2 *(so / because)* On Saturday morning the weather was rainy, so Ellie and I went to a café.

3 *(but / and)* We had a sandwich and an ice cream and we talked. It was good.

4 *(so / but)* After lunch, it was sunny, so we went to the Hoe.

5 *(because / but)* I like Plymouth, but I prefer Bath, where I live now.

6 *(and / because)* But I felt sad when I went home, because I miss my friends in Plymouth.

b) Complete John's sentences with **and/so/because/but**.

I'd like to join the music club at school because I love music. I play the drums, but I can't sing. I'm terrible! My favourite group is the Black Eyed Peas and my favourite singer is Jennifer Lopez. I like J.Lo because she's pretty and she's a good singer. I got money for my birthday, so/and I bought her new CD.

c) Write John's sentences.
Put the verbs in the simple past and use **and/so/because/but**.

You need more words for a correct sentence!

1 On Sunday morning / stay in bed / tired

On Sunday morning I stayed in bed because I was tired.

2 After lunch / weather sunny / play football in park

After lunch the weather was sunny, so I played football in the park.

3 Then / do homework / listen to music

Then I did my homework and listened to music.

4 After dinner / watch film on TV / a bit boring

After dinner I watched a film on TV, but it was a bit boring.

1020

▸ SB p. 21

21 WORDS The rules at your school

Write some *ideal* or *crazy* rules for your school! Use: have to / can / mustn't.

More help p. 85

Examples: Ideal – Teachers mustn't give students lots of homework.
Crazy – Students have to wear swimsuits in class!

1 ...

2 ...

3 ...

4 ... 1121

5 ...

▸ SB p. 22

22 MEDIATION A school trip

You and your partner are with a group of German students on a school exchange in Britain. Look at this poster about a school trip. Discuss the trip with your partner.
Ask and answer these questions in German:

Wohin?

Für wen?

Kosten?

Wann?

Treffpunkt?

Etwas mitbringen?

Bis wann eintragen?

Wann wieder abholen?

A trip to the beach

for all our German visitors and their British exchange partners!

All welcome!

The trip is free!

Date: Saturday 30th September

The bus leaves at 9 am. All students going on the trip must meet in front of the school at 8.30 am. Don't be late!

We will have a picnic on the beach, so you must bring a snack for lunch.

Do you want to come on the trip? You must write your name on this list before 4pm on Wednesday 28th.

After the trip, parents must pick you up at the school at 8.30pm.

Adam Johnson
Laura Macintosh

1123
1124

▸ SB p. 22

Das habe ich in Unit 1 gelernt:			
Meine Ergebnisse aus Stop! Check! Go! im Schülerbuch: ☺ 😐 ☹	**Ich kann …**	**Und wie gut bin ich darin wirklich?** ☺ 😐 ☹ **Selbsteinschätzung oder Lehrereinschätzung:**	**Frage deine Lehrerin oder deinen Lehrer nun nach passendem Übungsmaterial.**
S. 24 – S. 25 1 ○ 2 ○ 3 ○ 4 ○	1 … schreiben, was jemand in der Vergangenheit getan bzw. nicht getan hat *(simple past)*. S. 14 – S. 16	○	DFF 1.1 ⚀ DFF 1.1 ⚁ DFF 1.1 ⚂
S. 25 5 ○ 6 ○	2 … Regeln auf Englisch erklären. S. 22	○	DFF 1.2 ⚀ DFF 1.2 ⚁ DFF 1.2 ⚂
S. 26 7 ○	3 … sagen, was ich in meinen Ferien gemacht habe und andere danach fragen. S. 8, S. 10	○	DFF 1.3 ⚀ DFF 1.3 ⚁ DFF 1.3 ⚂
S. 27 8 ○	4 … einen Text über Vergangenes schreiben und überarbeiten. S. 21	○	DFF 1.4 ⚀ DFF 1.4 ⚁ DFF 1.4 ⚂
S. 27 9 ○	5 … einen Text über Vergangenes lesen und verstehen. S. 17 – S. 19	○	DFF 1.5 ⚀ DFF 1.5 ⚁ DFF 1.5 ⚂
Diese Fertigkeiten hast du auch geübt. Schätze selbst ein, wie gut du sie schon beherrschst.	6 … hören und verstehen, was andere in ihren Ferien gemacht haben. S. 9 – S. 10	○	DFF 1.6 ⚀ DFF 1.6 ⚁ DFF 1.6 ⚂
	7 … über Gefühle und Freundschaft sprechen. S. 19	○	DFF 1.7 ⚀ DFF 1.7 ⚁ DFF 1.7 ⚂
	8 … Methoden nutzen, um mir Wörter besser zu merken. S. 20	○	DFF 1.8 ⚀ DFF 1.8 ⚁ DFF 1.8 ⚂

Auf diesen Seiten im Schülerbuch findest du die Inhalte.

Auf den folgenden Seiten findest du weitere Übungen, die zu den Lernschwerpunkten passen.

Du kannst diese Seite auch in dein Dossier heften, wenn du fertig bist.

In der letzten Spalte können Sie die Schülerinnen und Schüler auf die individuell passenden Aufgaben im Material „Differenzieren Fördern Fordern“ verweisen. Wird z.B. die Beherrschung der zweiten Kompetenz in Unit 1 eher mit ☺ eingeschätzt, dann passt dazu das Material 1.2 ⚂. Wahlweise können Sie in diesen Feldern auch andere geeignete Übungsaufgaben benennen.

1 What they did in the holidays

p.88

Find the missing words (1–5), then find where Sarah went in the summer (6).

1 SWIMMING
2 SUMMER CAMP
3 LAKE
4 FAMILY BARBECUE
5 MOUNTAINS
6 (down) SPAIN

Joe — I went (1)  every day.

Amy — I went to a (2)  .

Fiona — We went camping near a (3)  . On my birthday we had a (4)  .

Ross — We went walking in the (5) 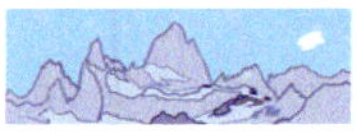 .

Sarah — We went to (6) Spain.

► SB p. 8

2 Luca's brother Jack sees his friend Wayne

p.88

a) Complete the dialogue, then read it with a partner.

Jack — Hi Wayne. Nice to see you again.

Wayne — Hi Jack. Give me five! How were your holidays?

Jack — They were OK, thanks. I stayed in bed late every day. What about you?

Wayne — I went to Turkey with my family in August. It was fun!

Jack — What was the weather like?

Wayne — It was hot and sunny. I didn't want to come home!

b) Imagine a dialogue about the holidays between you and a friend.

Exercise 2a) can help you.

Friend — ______________________________

You — ______________________________

Friend — ______________________________

You — ______________________________

Friend — ______________________________

You — ______________________________

► SB p. 10

p.88

3 Ellie's friend John talks about the holidays

Complete John's email. Put the verbs in the simple past.

In the holidays I *(go)* went to Scotland and *(stay)* stayed with my uncle in St Andrews. It *(be)* was great! I *(not know)* didn't know St Andrews before – I really *(like)* liked the town and I *(love)* loved the beach. My uncle *(buy)* bought a ball and we *(play)* played football on the beach every day. We *(have)* had lots of barbecues in the garden. I *(not miss)* didn't miss my friends – and I *(make)* made a new friend – my uncle's new dog! I *(not want)* didn't want to come home!

► SB p. 16

p.88

4 School clubs

a) Find clubs in the list for these six people and complete what they say.

After-school clubs this year:

Monday – music club (room 36); geography club (room 18)
Tuesday – art club (room 38); dance club (gym)
Wednesday – football club (gym); science club (room 23); ICT club (computer room)
Thursday – karate club (gym); cooking club (room 47)
Friday – book club (room 12); adventure club (meet in the gym)

I can't do my school work at home – my bedroom is too small and the house is too noisy. I'd like to join the homework club.
Emily

I play the drums and the saxophone, and really like singing. I'd like to join the music club.
Seb

I'm very interested in biology, and I like physics and chemistry too. I'd like to join the science club.
Caroline

I like sport very much. I play football and I go jogging every week. I'd like to try a new sport. I'd like to join the karate club.
Evan

I love reading – detective stories, adventure stories, science-fiction – everything! I'd like to join the book club.
Julia

I make breakfast for my family every Sunday. I'd like to learn to make different things. I'd like to join the cooking club.
Jason

b) Which club would you like to join – and why?

____

____

► SB p. 13

5 ★ FAST FINISHERS John's dream

p. 88

a) Read the text. Are the sentences right, wrong or is the information not in the text?

On Friday night I went to bed early because I was very tired. On Saturday morning I didn't get up early – I stayed in bed late and listened to my mp3 player. Then I had a fantastic surprise – Jennifer Lopez phoned me and invited me to have lunch with her. We had lunch at a really cool restaurant and we talked and laughed like old friends. I didn't feel nervous – she was really nice and I was very happy.

My dad bought a Ferrari, and after lunch he and I drove to Wembley. We didn't have to pay – we had free tickets. We watched our team, Bath City, against Chelsea. Bath is just a small football club, but we won 14– 0!! It was amazing!

Then in the evening, I went to a Black Eyed Peas concert and I met them all after the concert. They were so friendly!

Then I woke up[1] ... and it was Saturday morning. I thought "Oh no!". "Get up now, John!" said my mum. "We're going to the supermarket. You can help me."

	Right	Wrong	Not in the text
1 In the dream, John got up early on Saturday.		✓	
2 He had lunch with Jennifer Lopez.	✓		
3 He had chicken and chips for lunch.			✓
4 He went to Wembley by bus.		✓	
5 His favourite team won the football match.	✓		
6 He went to a concert on Sunday.		✓	
7 They played his favourite song at the concert.			✓

b) Now invent a dream for you! Write it on a piece of paper or in your exercise book.

Join sentences with *because, and, but, so.*

• Dein Traum kann so wild und unwahrscheinlich sein, wie du willst.
• Entscheide selbst, wie lang dein Text sein soll – hier hast du eine Gelegenheit zu zeigen, was du auf Englisch schreiben kannst.

Ideas:

On Saturday morning After lunch Then At ... o'clock In the evening ...	I (didn't) ... We	stay • help • listen • watch • play • skype • phone • text • visit • talk • invite • help get up • go • buy • come • see • feel • do • have (lunch) • feel • drive • make • eat • meet • win • have to • read • write

[1] I woke up *ich wachte auf*

Neighbours

1 In the street

a) Look at the picture. Write the right words.

1 newsagent	2 letterbox	3 car park
4 bus stop	5 map	6 traffic lights

1601

b) Write six sentences about the street your school is on:
There's a … / There are some … There isn't a … / There aren't any …

Use ideas from part a) and your own ideas.

► SB p. 29

2 In a British street: Quiz questions

a) Work with a partner. Do you know the answers? If not, guess!

1 When you cross the road in Britain, you must first look a) ☐ left b) ☑ right.

2 When you open a window in Britain, the window goes
a) ☐ into the room b) ☑ outside the house.

3 In British shops you buy things with a) ☐ shillings b) ☐ euros c) ☐ pounds.

4 In Britain, car drivers sit on the a) ☐ left b) ☑ right.

5 The colours of traffic lights in Britain are
a) ☑ red, orange and green b) ☐ red and green only.

6 London buses are a) ☐ white b) ☑ red c) ☐ yellow d) ☐ blue.

4 b) Listen and check your answers.

► SB p. 29

3 Words from the story

Find the missing words and put them in the word chain.

1 Half an hour later Adam and Mia came back – without Buster.

2 Adam shouted "Get lost!" to the kids in the street.

3 When he heard the firework, Buster was very scared.

4 Mrs Trent asked Mia: "Do you live around here?"

5 Adam had a new collar for Buster.

6 Adam said "Buster can't be very far away."

7 Buster ran away as fast as he could.

1 H							
A							
2 L	O	3 S	T				
F		C		5 C			
		4 A	R	O	U	N	D
		R		L			
		E		L		7 F	
		D		6 A	W	A	Y
				R		S	
						T	

► SB p. 31

4 Find the cat!

Write the words in the poster:

friendly • lost • missing • owner's • ran • reward • small • tail

MISSING !!

My cat ran away on Tuesday. Her name is Sooty. She's small and black and has a white tail. She likes people – she's very friendly. Can you find my lost cat?

Owner's phone number: 01724 388122. Reward: £25!

1704

► SB p. 31

5 Festivals

Luca tells Mia about Christmas in Plymouth. Write about a festival that **you** celebrate[1].

Christmas is on 25th December. We don't get any presents on 24th December, but on Christmas morning we find some presents next to our bed. That's always exciting! We usually stay at home on Christmas Day and we have a special lunch. We often play our favourite games and sometimes watch old films. Usually the weather is ...

Ideas:
Name? *(Karneval/Walpurgisnacht/Ramadan/...?)* When?
Is it fun/exciting/boring?
Do you always/usually/sometimes/often ... sing some songs / play some games / visit people / get lots of presents / eat and drink some special things / ...?
What *don't* you do? (e.g. don't give any presents)

► SB p. 31

[1] celebrate *feiern*

6 Dogs

Complete the word web with your ideas.

Ideas:
short tail • collar • run in fields • play with our neighbour's dog • need time with their owner

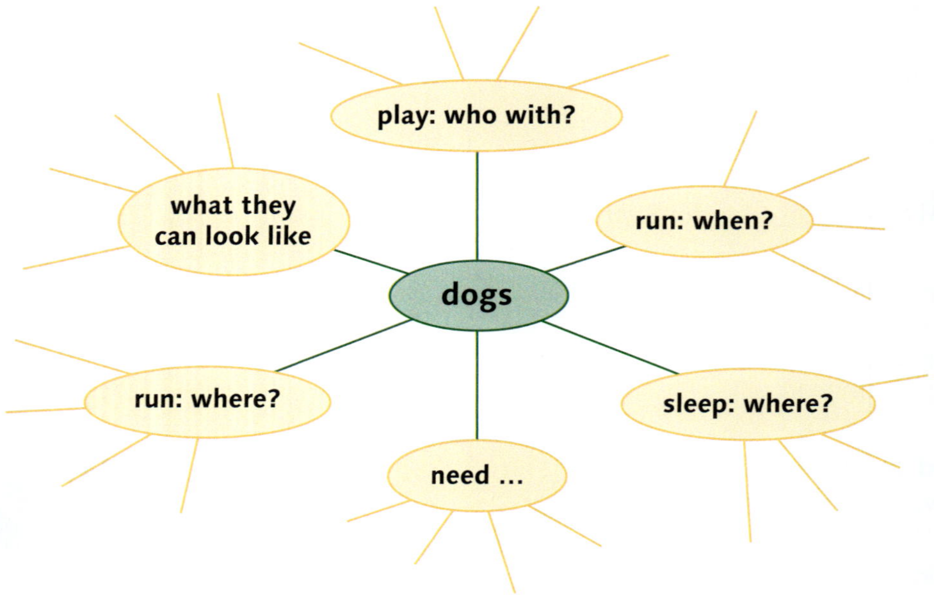

► SB p. 33

7 The right pet

A reader writes to a pet magazine. Read his letter and write an answer for him:
– Why is a dog not a good pet for Alan and his family?
– What do you think is a good pet for Alan? Why?

Dear *Pet Fun*,
I don't have any pets, but I'd like a dog. We have a small flat and we don't have a garden. My dad doesn't like animals and my mum doesn't like lots of noise. Mum and Dad work all day and I'm at school. What's a good pet for my family?
Alan

Ideas:
a (dog) needs ... • you have to ... • your family doesn't have ...

…

…

…

…

…

► SB p. 33

8 A class game

a) Complete the questions (1–15) with the verbs in the box.

b) Write three more questions (16–18).

check • ~~eat~~ • go • have • listen • make • play • sing • stop • take • talk • text • walk • watch • wear

1. *Did* you *eat* potatoes yesterday?
Name: ______

2. *Did* you *sing* a song yesterday?
Name: ______

3. *Did* you *watch* sport on TV yesterday?
Name: ______

4. *Did* you *walk* to school yesterday?
Name: ______

5. *Did* you *stop* at a traffic light yesterday?
Name: ______

6. *Did* you *take* a photo yesterday?
Name: ______

7. *Did* you *wear* jeans yesterday?
Name: ______

8. *Did* you *have* breakfast yesterday?
Name: ______

9. *Did* you *go* to a friend's house or flat yesterday?
Name: ______

10. *Did* you *listen* to the radio yesterday?
Name: ______

11. *Did* you *text* a friend yesterday?
Name: ______

12. *Did* you *talk* to your grandma yesterday?
Name: ______

13. *Did* you *play* a musical instrument yesterday?
Name: ______

14. *Did* you *make* dinner for the family yesterday?
Name: ______

15. *Did* you *check* the internet yesterday?
Name: ______

16. ______
______
Name: ______

17. ______
______
Name: ______

18. ______
______
Name: ______

c) Play the game! Walk round the class. Ask a student a question.
- If the student says *No, I didn't* – ask another question.
- If the student says *Yes, I did* – write his/her name. Then ask a different student a question.

1908

The winner is • the first student with a name in all boxes *or*
• the student with the most names when the teacher ends the game.

▸ SB p. 36

9 Last year's Guy Fawkes party

a) Look at the answers on the right. Then write the right question words.

How • What • When • Where • Who • Why

1 Where did you have your party? – In Drake's Park.

2 Who came to the party? – We all came: Luca and his family, Berry and her family, etc.

3 What did you eat at the party? – We ate sausages and potatoes, yummy!

4 When did the party finish? – It finished at ten o'clock.

5 How did you go to the party? – We went by bus.

6 Why did you have the party in a park? – Because we didn't have space for everybody in the garden.

b) Write the verbs in the simple past in Ellie's answers.
Then write a good question for each answer! *"Did you ...?"*

Questions	Ellie's answers
1 Did you wear a costume?	Yes, I wore a witch costume. *(wear)*
2 Did you eat (sausages)?	No, I ate chocolate biscuits. *(eat)*
3 Did you drink (lemonade)?	No, we drank cocoa because it was cold. *(drink)*
4 Did someone play the guitar?	Yes, my friend's dad played the guitar. *(play)*
5 Did you sing songs?	Yes, we sang lots of songs. *(sing)*
6 Did you have fireworks?	Yes, we had really great fireworks. *(have)*

2009

► *SB p. 36*

10 Mia's time in Germany

Circle the right form of the verb.

Ellie ___ Where do / did you live / lived when you were in Germany?

Mia ___ We live / lived in Leipzig, that's a big city.

Ellie ___ Do / Did you often go / went to the city centre?

Mia ___ Yes, we go / went quite often.

Ellie ___ What do / did you do / did there?

Mia ___ Oh, I go / went shopping, or I visit / visited friends. Leipzig is a great place!

2010

► *SB p. 35*

11 Last weekend

a) Write six questions for your partner about last weekend.

Look at your Language files on page 93 for help.

Ideas:
Did ...? • Where/When/What/Who/How ... did ...?
go • get up • wear • see • eat • watch • go to bed • stay • visit

1 ...

2 ...

3 ...

4 ...

5 ...

6 ...

b) Now ask your partner your questions.
Your partner answers – but their answers can be true or false!
Can you guess if an answer is true or false? You get one point[1] if you're right!
Then your partner asks you. Who has more points at the end – you or your partner?

► SB p. 35

12 Angry parents

a) What are the parents asking?
With a partner, write four questions and invent[2] the boy's answers.

Example: Why did you go out in this weather?!
And why ...?! Where ...?! Who ...?! What ...?!

... ...

b) Then act the scene!

► SB p. 35

[1] point *Punkt* [2] invent *erfinden*

13 Questions about the story

a) Answer the questions. Write sentences.

1 What did Mia and Ellie want money for? They wanted it for the dogs' home.

2 How much money did they get? They got £8.50.

3 Who took the money? Two boys took the money.

4 Why didn't the girls see their faces? The boys had/wore masks.

5 The girls saw the boys later. Where were they? They were in front of a shop.

6 Who got the money from the boys? Buster got the money.

7 Where did the friends go in the evening? They went to a bonfire party.

b) ● Write three more questions about the story and ask your partner. Can he/she answer?

1 ______

2 ______

3 ______

2213

▸ SB p. 39

14 Words in the story

Two boys took the money.

Write the words (1–7) in the puzzle and find out what they were called (8 & 9):

8 Mark and

9 Joe

							1 S	**M**	I	L	E	
							2 P	**A**	P	E	R	
3 P	U	S	H	C	H	A	I	**R**				
					4 B	A	R	**K**	S			

	5 **J**	A	C	K	E	T
6 P	**O**	C	K	E	T	
7 H	**E**	A	D			

1 You do this (with your mouth!) when you're happy.

2 You read this when you want to know the news.

3 Ellie's baby brother sits in this when Alisha goes out with him.

4 A dog doesn't speak – it does this!

5 When it's cold, you wear a pullover – and this too!

6 You can keep money in this in your trousers.

7 You wear a hat on this.

2214

▸ SB p. 39

15 Instructions

a) Read the instructions and do what they tell you.

> Always read all the instructions! What exactly do you have to do?

1 Read instructions 1–9 before you write or draw.
2 Draw a dog in the space on the right.
3 Colour the dog black.
4 Give the dog brown ears.
5 Draw a hat for the dog.
6 Write five things that dogs eat: *dog biscuits, ...*
7 Write a good name for the dog.
8 Don't do the instructions 2–7.
9 Draw fireworks in the space on the right.

b) Now compare with a partner. Did you do the same thing?

2315

▸ SB p. 40

16 LISTENING A trip to Bristol

5

a) A group of students from Plymouth went to Bristol by train. They visited a museum and then they went shopping in town. At 3.30 pm they met for their train back to Plymouth. But there was a problem …

- Listen to the CD.
- Tick the right options a, b, c or d.
- One or two options can be right.
- You will hear the recording twice.

> Read the instructions and all the questions before you start. How many answers can you tick?

1 There were a) ☐ 14 b) ☐ 15 c) ☐ 16 d) ✓ 18 students in the group.

2 Anna was with Charlotte a) ☐ at the post office. b) ✓ in a milk shake bar. c) ☐ in a fruit and veg shop. d) ✓ at the market.

3 Anna last saw Charlotte at a) ☐ two o'clock. b) ☐ two thirty. c) ✓ three o'clock. d) ☐ three thirty.

4 Gavin saw Charlotte a) ☐ at the newsagent's. b) ☐ at the letterbox. c) ✓ at the traffic lights. d) ✓ near the car park.

5 In the end a) ✓ Charlotte came. b) ☐ Charlotte missed the train. c) ☐ the students missed their train. d) ✓ all was OK.

2316

6

b) How many answers did you tick? Listen and check your answers.

▸ SB p. 40

17 WRITING A letter or email about a party or festival

a) Here is a task in a test. Read the instructions, but don't start writing yet.

- Write a short letter or email to your English penfriend, Jimmy.
- Tell him three things about a party or festival you went to last week, last month, etc.
- Ask Jimmy two questions about what he did last weekend.
- Write at least 60 words.

b) Imagine you are the teacher. Read what one student wrote and tick 'yes' or 'no' in 1–6.

Dear Jimmy,

How are you? I want to tell you about my birthday party. It was on Saturday.

I invited four friends and we played our favourite games. Then we had some food, and in the evening we watched two films. We had a great time.

What did you do on your birthday?

Simon

1 The start of the letter is OK.
☑ Yes ☐ No

2 The letter says at least two things about a party or festival.
☑ Yes ☐ No

3 The letter asks three questions about last weekend.
☐ Yes ☑ No

4 Simon uses time phrases and linking words.
☑ Yes ☐ No

5 The end of the letter is OK.
☐ Yes ☑ No

6 The letter has at least 50 words.
☑ Yes ☐ No

c) Now write your letter or email.

comments:

... ______________________ ______________

... ______________________ ______________

... ______________________ ______________

... ______________________ ______________

... ______________________ ______________

... ______________________ ______________

2417

d) Now look at your partner's letter or email.
Does it follow the instructions? Write *comments* like in b).

Example: The start of the letter is OK.

► SB p. 41

7 18 A tourist in London

Big Ben • Buckingham Palace • Hyde Park • the London Eye • the Science Museum • Tower Bridge

a) Look at these places in London. Can you write the right names? Then listen and check.

1

Big Ben

2

the London Eye

3

the Science Museum

4

Tower Bridge

5

Buckingham Palace

6

Hyde Park

b) Complete this dialogue with a tourist in London. Write the missing words.

Tourist Excuse me, please. I'm looking for Big Ben. Can you tell me the way, please?

Woman Big Ben? Let me see. Go along Waterloo Road and cross Waterloo Bridge.

Tourist Waterloo Bridge. OK.

Woman Then turn left into The Strand, and then turn left into Whitehall. Big Ben is on the left.

Tourist Thank you.

Woman You're welcome.

8 c) LISTENING Now listen to the dialogue and check your answers in b).

9 d) LISTENING Now look at the map of London on the next page. You are at X on the map. Listen to the instructions. Write the names of the places on the map.

e) SPEAKING Partner work
Partner A: You're at X on the map. Tell your partner the way to one of the places.
Partner B: You're at X on the map. Listen to your partner's instructions. Where do you go?
• Then swap roles.

2518

▸ SB p. 42

A *the London Eye*

B *Tower Bridge*

C *Big Ben*

D *Buckingham Palace*

E *Science Museum*

F *Hyde Park*

2619
2620

Das habe ich in Unit 2 gelernt:			
Meine Ergebnisse aus Stop! Check! Go! im Schülerbuch: ☺ 😐 ☹	Ich kann …	Und wie gut bin ich darin wirklich? ☺ 😐 ☹ Selbsteinschätzung oder Lehrereinschätzung:	Frage deine Lehrerin oder deinen Lehrer nun nach passendem Übungsmaterial.
S. 44 – S. 45 2 ○ 4 ○	1 … Fragen zu Ereignissen in der Vergangenheit stellen und darauf antworten. S. 34 – S. 36	○	DFF 2.1 ⚀ DFF 2.1 ⚁ DFF 2.1 ⚂
S. 45 5 ○	2 … Wortverbindungen herstellen. S. 34 – S. 35	○	DFF 2.2 ⚀ DFF 2.2 ⚁ DFF 2.2 ⚂
S. 45 6 ○	3 … jemandem etwas anbieten (*some* und *any*). S. 30	○	DFF 2.3 ⚀ DFF 2.3 ⚁ DFF 2.3 ⚂
S. 46 7 ○	4 … Wegbeschreibungen verstehen und jemandem den Weg erklären. S. 42	○	DFF 2.4 ⚀ DFF 2.4 ⚁ DFF 2.4 ⚂
S. 46 8 ○	5 … einen Brief über ein Ereignis schreiben. S. 41	○	DFF 2.5 ⚀ DFF 2.5 ⚁ DFF 2.5 ⚂
	6 … kulturelle Unterschiede zwischen Großbritannien und Deutschland benennen. S. 28 , S. 30	○	DFF 2.6 ⚀ DFF 2.6 ⚁ DFF 2.6 ⚂
Diese Fertigkeiten hast du auch geübt. Schätze selbst ein, wie gut du sie schon beherrschst.	7 … Dinge in einer Wohngegend benennen und darüber berichten. S. 28 – S. 29	○	DFF 2.7 ⚀ DFF 2.7 ⚁ DFF 2.7 ⚂
	8 … einem Text Informationen zu Haustieren entnehmen. S. 32 – S. 33	○	DFF 2.8 ⚀ DFF 2.8 ⚁ DFF 2.8 ⚂
	9 … Testaufgaben bewältigen. S. 40 – S. 41	○	DFF 2.9 ⚀ DFF 2.9 ⚁ DFF 2.9 ⚂

Auf diesen Seiten im Schülerbuch findest du die Inhalte.

Auf den folgenden Seiten findest du weitere Übungen, die zu den Lernschwerpunkten passen.

Du kannst diese Seite auch in dein Dossier heften, wenn du fertig bist.

Bitte beachten Sie auf Seite 12 den Hinweis zur Verwendung der Materialien aus „Differenzieren Fördern Fordern“, die sich nach dieser Einschätzung anbietet.

STOP AND PRACTISE

p. 88

1 A guy for Guy Fawkes day

John and his friends made a guy. What clothes did they collect? Write the words.

hat
mask
pullover
jacket
trainers
shirt
trousers

p. 89

2 John asks for directions

a) Write the missing words in the dialogue and in the puzzle.

– (11) Excuse me, please. Is there a newsagent's (10) near (6) here ?

– Yes, (7 ↓) there' s a newsagent's in Blake Street.

– Can you tell me the (1) way , please?

– Yes, go (2) along Moss Street and go (9) past the post office. Then (7 →) turn right into Blake Street. (3) Cross Blake Street at the traffic (5) lights . The newsagent's is (4) on the left.

– Great. Thanks very (8) much .

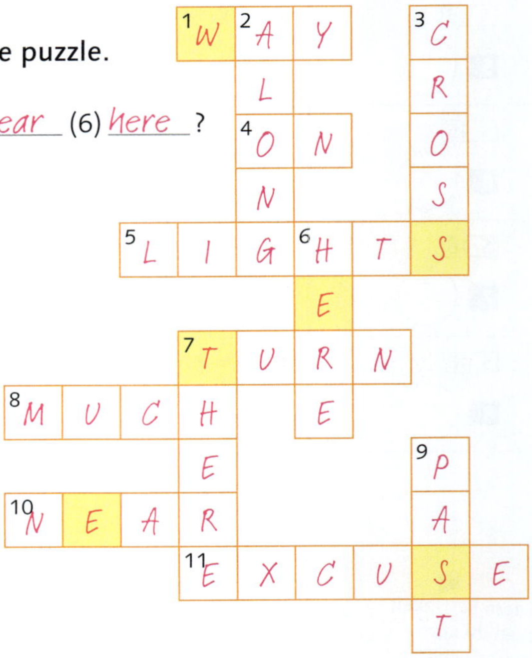

b) What does John buy at the newsagent's?

– He buys sweets .

▸ SB p. 42

p. 89

3 Last Sunday

Write the questions – and your answers.

Make your answers as long as possible!

1 Q when get up Sunday? When did you get up on Sunday?

A ...

2 Q what do morning? What did you do in the morning?

A ...

3 Q where have lunch? Where did you have lunch?

A ...

▸ SB p. 42

4 A singer's Saturday

p. 89

a) Complete the sentences with the correct form of the simple past.

On Saturday morning I usually go to the gym, but last Saturday I *(not go)* didn't go there because I had a concert in the evening. I *(have)* had lunch at a top restaurant with my friends, but I *(not drink)* didn't drink any alcohol because I *(want)* wanted to be at my best for the concert. I *(not do)* didn't do anything in the afternoon – I just *(stay)* stayed at home and *(listen)* listened to music, (but I *(not listen)* didn't listen to my own music!).

In the evening, I *(go)* went to the theatre for the concert. Usually I feel very nervous, but this time I only *(feel)* felt a bit nervous – then I *(see)* saw the audience! There were thousands of fans! I *(sing)* sang really well and the concert *(be)* was great – the fans *(not want)* didn't want it to finish! I *(have)* had a really great time.

I usually get up at about 8am, but on Sunday I was really tired, so I *(not get up)* didn't get up early. I *(stay)* stayed in bed all morning and *(get up)* got up at lunchtime.

b) ★ FAST FINISHERS Imagine you're a pop superstar / an actor / a sports star. Write about last Saturday:

Ideas:
Who are you?
Do you usually stay at home / go out (who with)?
Which stars do you know/see?
What did you do last Saturday?
Did you have a concert / a match?
Did you sing/play well? How many fans came?
How many goals did you score[1]? How did you feel?

[1] score a goal *Tore schießen*

Unit 3 Teen talk

1 What can you do at the weekend?

a) Work with a partner. Write as many ideas as you can.

1 I like watching a DVD, a good film, my favourite TV programme, etc.

2 I like doing a hobby, sport, chores, the shopping, etc.

3 I like chilling alone, with friends, with my sister, etc.

in the garden, in my bedroom, in the living room,etc.

4 I like going to the cinema, the zoo, my friend's house, etc.

5 I like playing the guitar, football, with my dog, etc.

6 I like visiting my grandparents, caves, nice places, etc.

3001

b) Now read your answers in class.
You get one point for each idea if nobody else have it. Which pair get the most points?

Our points: ________

▸ SB p. 49

2 What did Ellie do at the weekend?

- Write sentences.
- Use one time phrase in each sentence:

✓ = she did this
✗ = she didn't do this

More help p. 85

… 10 am • … afternoon • before … • after … • … Sunday • … weekend • … evening

1 ✓  She went shopping / to the shops at 10 am.

2 ✓  She listened to music in the afternoon.

3 ✓  She did chores before dinner.

4 ✗  She didn't go swimming on Sunday.

5 ✗  She didn't meet friends at the weekend.

6 ✗  She didn't do stuff on the internet/computer after lunch.

▸ SB p. 49

3 What chores do they do?

10

a) Listen to six teenagers in Ellie's class. What chores do they do at home? Look at the pictures and write the letters.

First, get ready! Look at the pictures – what are the chores in English? Then listen and do the exercise. You can hear the text a second time.

A

B

C

D

E

F

G

H

1 Sophie [E] + [C]   2 John [H] + [D]   3 Samantha [A] + [G]

4 Olivia [F] + [E]   5 Harry [G] + [B] + [D]   6 James [E]

b) When do the six teenagers help at home? Look at sentences 1–6. Then listen again and write 1–6 in the boxes.

1 When I've made a mess.
2 When Mum asks him/her.
3 When Mum and Dad have long days at work.
4 When Mum shouts at him/her.
5 When Dad is busy.
6 When he/she needs money.

3103

1 Sophie [3]   2 John [5]   3 Samantha [2]   4 Olivia [1]   5 Harry [6]   6 James [4]

▸ SB p. 51

4 Chores in your house

a) Who does the chores in your house? Write at least three sentences.

Ideas:
My brother and I usually clean our rooms, but Mum sometimes does it if it's too bad!
My dad often goes to the supermarket because the supermarket is near the hospital where he works.

b) Who does the most[1] chores? Do you think it's fair?

▸ SB p. 51

[1] the most *die meisten*

5 Teens and money

Do a money survey in your class.

a) Talk to lots of students – as many as you can. Ask them the questions in the table below:

	1 Do you get pocket money?	2 Do you have a job? If yes, what do you do?	3 Do you do chores at home? If yes, what chores do you do?	4 What do you need money for?
Student 1 ______				
Student 2 ______				
Student 3 ______				
Student 4 ______				
Student 5 ______				

b) Now write about the results[1]. You can use these ideas to help you:

More help p. 86

Ideas:
money survey in our class
I talked to ... students in our class. • Five students ... • Three students ... • I'm surprised because (only one student ...) • All students need money for ... and some need money for ...

You can put your text in your dossier.

► SB p. 51

6 Which do you like?

Point at the clothes and talk about them with a partner. Use *this/that* and *these/those*.

Do you like this *hoodie* or that *hoodie*?

I like this *hoodie*.

This *hoodie*? Why?

Because that *hoodie* is too grey!

3206

► SB p. 52

[1] result *Ergebnis*

7 Ellie wants to buy a toy for Finn

a) Look at the picture and read the sentences. Find the right names for the teddy bears.

Cutie	Vlad	Teddy	Ted	Bob	Super-Ted

1 Teddy is cheaper than Ted.
2 Vlad is scarier than the others.
3 Super-Ted is more expensive than Vlad.
4 Bob is smaller than Super-Ted, but bigger than Ted.
5 Cutie is smaller and cuter than all the others.

b) Which teddy bear would you buy for Ellie's baby brother? ______

Why? ______

______

► SB p. 55

8 What do you think?

a) Write sentences. Say what you think.

bad • funny • good • interesting • popular • scary

You find the rules on WB p. 94 (LF 12).

1 a hamster / a monkey

I think a ______ is funnier than a ______

2 technology / drama

... is more interesting than ...

3 Dracula / Frankenstein

... is scarier ...

4 orange juice / cola

... is more popular than ...

5 the town / the country

... is better than ...

3308

6 shopping / doing chores

... is worse than ...

► SB p. 55

b) Write 4 sentences. Write what you think – and why.

Example: I think ... is/are ... than ... because ...

1

(I think a mobile is more useful than a phone because it has a camera and games.

2

I think books are more popular than e-readers because they're cheaper.)

(I think a dog is better than a cat because you can run and play with a dog.

4

I think maths is easier than geography because I like maths better.)

► SB p. 55

9 Animal quiz

Complete the questions with words from the box. Then do the quiz.

dangerous • big • fast • lazy • noisy • small

You find the answers on page 90.

1 The noisiest animal in the world is the blue whale.[1]
You can hear it ... a) ☐ 8.5 km b) ☐ 85 km c) ☑ 850 km ... away.

2 The fastest animal on land can run at 113 km/h. What is it?
a) ☐ the leopard b) ☑ the cheetah[2] c) ☐ the gazelle

3 The laziest animal in the world sleeps for 22–23 hours a day!
It's ... a) ☐ the crocodile b) ☐ the python c) ☑ the koala.

4 The world's smallest dog is only ... a) ☑ 10 cm b) ☐ 15 cm c) ☐ 20 cm tall.

5 The world's biggest animal weighs[3] more than 100 tonnes. What is it?
a) ☑ the blue whale b) ☐ the elephant c) ☐ the giraffe

6 The world's most dangerous animal is ... a) ☐ the tiger b) ☐ the lion[4]
c) ☑ the mosquito[5] – about two million people die every year.

3409

► SB p. 56

[1] blue whale *Blauwal* [2] cheetah *Gepard* [3] weigh *wiegen* [4] lion *Löwe* [5] mosquito *Stechmücke*

10 Tell the story.

You can colour each sentence.

a) Draw arrows and tell the story.

Luca was at home	because he didn't have	liked Luca's den	and had a 90s party.
He helped his dad tidy	any money to go out.	surprised. They really	arrived, they were
the garage for £7.50.	to a charity shop, and	got money for the CDs	When his friends
They found lots of	plan. They gave things	at a second-hand CD	garage and made a den.
rubbish, but also things	to recycle. Luca had a	shop. Luca put the sofa	and things back in the

3510

b) Then read the sentences to your partner.

► SB p. 59

11 What do you think?

Write why the things happened.

1 Why couldn't Luca do more interesting things at the weekend?

Because he didn't have any money.

2 Why did Luca and his dad go to the Oxfam shop?

Because they wanted to give the shop lots of old things.

3 Why was Luca's dad surprised in the second-hand shop?

Because he got £25 for the old CDs.

4 Why didn't the woman in the shop take all CDs?

Because she liked the other CDs better than the Spice Girls.

5 Was Luca poor at the end of the story? Why (not)?

I think he wasn't poor because he had some money.

► SB p. 59

12 Your perfect den

Think about your perfect den. What does it look like?
What do you / don't you have in it?
Describe it!

Ideas:
The walls are … (blue). • There's a big …
You can … (dance) in it.

► SB p. 59

13 LISTENING What's your hobby?

11 Listen to two teenagers. Write the details in the table.

	Lexi	Jacob
Hobby	karting[1]	cooking
When he/she does it	not very often	every Sunday
Who with?	friends	his dad
Where?	a farm	kitchen / at home
The problem is ...	it's expensive	kitchen gets messy
Why he/she likes it	it's exciting	likes nice food

3613

► SB p. 60

14 READING 'Hobbies' magazine

a) Read the magazine article. Colour the clown's costume.

Reader Paul Smith (14) tells us about his interesting hobby

Clowning about

I have a hobby which I love – I'm a clown! I first saw clowns when I went to a circus for my eighth birthday, and I started doing funny things at home. I made my little sister laugh.

Now I go to children's birthday parties. I do magic tricks, I make animals from balloons, I juggle, and I just do funny tricks and silly things. The kids love it (and the adults laugh too!). I love being a clown because you can make people laugh.

I have a great clown costume. I bought my blue jacket at a charity shop, so it was really cheap, and my mum made my trousers for me. They're red and yellow and very big. The most expensive part of my costume were the big long black clown shoes. I bought them from a special costume shop. And of course I have an orange wig and a big red nose!

Paul

b) Tick (✓) the right answer.

	right	wrong	not in the text
1 He first saw clowns on TV.		✓	
2 Now, he's a clown for children at birthday parties.	✓		
3 Paul goes to a party every month.			✓
4 He likes making people laugh.	✓		
5 Paul's sister is a clown now too.			✓
6 Paul made his clown trousers.		✓	

3614

c) Ask your partner four questions about Paul's hobby. Your partner answers. Then swap roles.

► SB p. 61

[1] karting *Gokart fahren*

15 WRITING An email about a hobby

a) Here is a task in a test. Read the instructions.

> Write an email to your English penfriend, Jimmy.
> Tell him about a hobby that you have:
> – what the hobby is
> – three things about it (ideas: when/where you do it; who with; why you like it)
> – Say what the problem is with your hobby.
> Ask Jimmy two questions about his hobby.
> Write at least 80 words.

b) Now write your email. More help p. 86

You can invent[1] the details if you want!

You can look at the tips in Unit 2 (on page 41 in your book).

How do you start a letter or email?

How many things must you say about your hobby?

The problem with your hobby?

Remember to ask two questions.

Is your email at least 80 words?

How do you end a letter or email?

c) Partner check: Look at your partner's email. You are the teacher! Tick (✓) Yes or No.

	Yes	No
1 The start of the email is OK.		
2 The email says at least three things about a hobby.		
3 The email asks a question about Jimmy's hobby.		
4 The end of the email is OK.		
5 The email has at least 80 words.		

3715

► SB p. 61

[1] invent *erfinden*

16 SPEAKING TV programmes

cartoon • comedy show • crime series • documentary • film • music show • news and weather • quiz show • reality show • soap • sports show • talk show

PARTNER A

a) Look at the list of TV programmes for BBC 1. Write what kind of TV programmes they are:

BBC 1	ITV 1
7.00 pm Pointless A quiz show with a difference – who can score the least points? Presented by Alexander Armstrong. quiz show	**7.00 pm** soap
7.30 pm Wanted Down Under A British family lives in Australia for a week to help them decide: do they want to emigrate? reality show	**7.30 pm** soap
8.00 pm Jungles Tonight's programme looks at the animals and birds of tropical rainforests. documentary	**8.00 pm** comedy show
9.00 pm Lewis An actor dies at the theatre. Who is the killer? Another mystery for Inspector Lewis. crime series	**9.00 pm** talk show
10.00 pm Match of the Day Join Gary Lineker for the best of the Premier League football action. sports show	**10.00 pm** film

b) Your partner has information about ITV 1 programmes. Ask questions and complete the list.

Example: *A* ___ What's on ITV 1 at 7 pm?
B ___ There's a soap. What's on BBC 1?
A ___ There's a quiz show.

c) Now decide[1] what to do! This dialogue helps you: change the blue words.

B ___ At 7 pm there's a soap and a quiz show.
A ___ I prefer soaps – let's watch that.
OR I don't like soaps or quiz shows. What about you?
B ___ OK, I like soaps too.
OR I don't really like soaps / soaps or quiz shows.
Why don't we listen to music at 7 o'clock?
A ___ Great. Now, at 7.30 there's a …

Your idea! Think of other activities!

► SB p. 62

[1] decide *entscheiden*

SPEAKING TV programmes

PARTNER B

a) Look at the list of TV programmes for ITV 1.
Write what kind of TV programmes they are:

cartoon • comedy show • crime series • documentary • film • music show • news and weather • quiz show • reality show • soap • sports show • talk show

BBC 1	ITV 1
7.00 pm quiz show	7.00 pm **Emerdale** Sandy looks for a place to live. Debbie has a plan to win Andy's love. soap
7.30 pm reality show	7.30 pm **Coronation Street** Tyrone sees his doctor – and gets bad news. Becky gets a shock at Danny's house. soap
8.00 pm documentary	8.00 pm **You've Been Framed** More funny videos sent in by the public. Presented by comedian Harry Hill. comedy show
9.00 pm crime series	9.00 pm **The Jonathan Ross Show** Ross talks to stars Robin Williams and Elle Macpherson. talk show
10.00 pm sports show	10.00 pm **Jurassic Park** Spielberg's classic dinosaur movie. film

b) Your partner has information about BBC 1 programmes. Ask questions and complete the list.

Example: A ___ What's on ITV 1 at 7 pm?
B ___ There's a soap. What's on BBC 1?
A ___ There's a quiz show.

c) Now decide[1] what to do! This dialogue helps you: change the blue words.

B ___ At 7 pm there's a soap and a quiz show.
A ___ I prefer soaps – let's watch that.
OR I don't like soaps or quiz shows. What about you?
B ___ OK, I like soaps too.
OR I don't really like soaps / soaps or quiz shows.
Why don't we listen to music at 7 o'clock?
A ___ Great. Now, at 7.30 there's a ...

Your idea! Think of other activities!

► SB p. 62

3916
3917
3918

[1] decide *entscheiden*

Das habe ich in Unit 3 gelernt:			
Meine Ergebnisse aus **Stop! Check! Go!** im Schülerbuch: ☺ 😐 ☹	Ich kann …	Und wie gut bin ich darin wirklich? ☺ 😐 ☹ Selbsteinschätzung oder Lehrereinschätzung:	Frage deine Lehrerin oder deinen Lehrer nun nach passendem Übungsmaterial.
S. 64 – 1b ◯ – 1c ◯	**1** … über meine Aufgaben zu Hause berichten. S. 51	◯	DFF 3.1 ⚀ DFF 3.1 ⚁ DFF 3.1 ⚂
S. 65 – 3 ◯	**2** … Dinge vergleichen *(comparatives)*. S. 54 – S. 55	◯	DFF 3.2 ⚀ DFF 3.2 ⚁ DFF 3.2 ⚂
S. 65 – 4a ◯	**3** … ein Interview verstehen und Notizen dazu machen. S. 50	◯	DFF 3.3 ⚀ DFF 3.3 ⚁ DFF 3.3 ⚂
S. 65 – 4c ◯	**4** … einen Kurzvortrag halten. S. 60 – S. 61	◯	DFF 3.4 ⚀ DFF 3.4 ⚁ DFF 3.4 ⚂
S. 66 – 5 ◯	**5** … einen Textausschnitt verstehen und Fragen dazu beantworten. S. 57 – S. 59	◯	DFF 3.5 ⚀ DFF 3.5 ⚁ DFF 3.5 ⚂
S. 66 – 6 ◯	**6** … Informationen vergleichen *(superlatives)*. S. 56	◯	DFF 3.6 ⚀ DFF 3.6 ⚁ DFF 3.6 ⚂
S. 67 – 8 ◯	**7** … zwischen einem deutschen und einem englischen Gesprächspartner eine Wochenendverabredung vermitteln. S. 53	◯	DFF 3.7 ⚀ DFF 3.7 ⚁ DFF 3.7 ⚂
	8 … über Kleidung sprechen. S. 52 – S. 53	◯	DFF 3.8 ⚀ DFF 3.8 ⚁ DFF 3.8 ⚂
	9 … kann Hinweise geben *(this/that/these/those)*. S. 52 – S. 53	◯	DFF 3.9 ⚀ DFF 3.9 ⚁ DFF 3.9 ⚂

Diese Fertigkeiten hast du auch geübt. Schätze selbst ein, wie gut du sie schon beherrschst.

Auf diesen Seiten im Schülerbuch findest du die Inhalte.

Auf den folgenden Seiten findest du weitere Übungen, die zu den Lernschwerpunkten passen.

Du kannst diese Seite auch in dein Dossier heften, wenn du fertig bist.

Bitte beachten Sie auf Seite 12 den Hinweis zur Verwendung der Materialien aus „Differenzieren Fördern Fordern“, die sich nach dieser Einschätzung anbietet.

Is chilling a sport?
Is shopping a hobby?
You decide!

p. 89

1 An alphabet of sports and hobbies

Work with a partner. Can you complete the alphabet?

Abseiling, b*adminton*  c*hilling*, d*arts* , extreme ironing, f*ootball*, g*ames* , h*ockey* , i*ce skating*, j*ogging* , karting, line *dancing* , m*eeting* friends, net*ball*, outdoor sports, p*op concerts*, quizzes, r*ugby* , s*wimming*, t*aking photos* , underwater swimming, v*olleyball*, w*atching TV*, xylophone, yachting, *zoo* visits.

▸ SB p. 49

p. 89

2 TV in Germany

a) What do you think? What are the best programmes on German TV? Write sentences.

1 good – music programme

The best music programme is …

2 exciting – crime series

The most exciting crime series is …

3 funny – comedy show

The funniest comedy show is …

4 popular – soap

The most popular soap is …

5 boring – programme

The most boring programme is …

6 good – reality show

The best reality show is …

7 interesting – documentary

The most interesting documentary is …

8 bad – TV programme

The worst TV programme is …

b) Does your partner agree? Ask him/her.

Partner A I think the best music programme is … What do you think?
Partner B I agree. / I don't agree. I think … is better.
I think the most exciting crime series is … What about you?

▸ SB p. 56, 62

p. 90

3 In your town or village

You're going to walk through your town/village and show places to an English friend. Prepare sentences like this about five places in your town or village.

Example: This is the sports centre where I play badminton every Tuesday evening.

This/That	is the *school/bus stop/shop/place/...* where ...	
This/That	is	the *best/worst/biggest/most popular/...* in ...
These/Those	are	

(This is the school where I went when I was small. Those are the oldest houses in our village. That's the bus stop where I get the bus every morning. These are the best pizzas in town!)

▸ SB p. 52, 56

p. 90

4 An interview about chores

a) Write five questions for people in your class.

	Answers – *some examples*					
	✓✓ Yes, I ... quite often / every day ✓ Yes, I sometimes ... ✗ No, I never ...			☺ It's OK / I like it ☹ I hate it! / It's (quite) boring ✗ We don't have a ... (garden)		
	1	2	3	1	2	3
Do you hoover the house?	☐	☐	☐	☐	☐	☐
Do you fill the dishwasher?	☐	☐	☐	☐	☐	☐
Do you clean the bathroom?	☐	☐	☐	☐	☐	☐
Do you cut the grass?	☐	☐	☐	☐	☐	☐
Do you wash up?	☐	☐	☐	☐	☐	☐

b) Ask three people the questions. Then ask: *How do you like it?*
Write their answers: ✓✓ / ✓ / ✗ / ☺ / ☹ / ✗

1 Do you hoover the house?

☹ Yes, I sometimes hoover the house, but it's boring.

c) Which chore do people hate the most?

▸ SB p. 51

5 A scary hobby

p.90

Read the text about Jack's hobby. Read the questions and complete the answers.

Jack Bruce, 25, has an unusual hobby. By day, he works in a post office, but in the evenings in summer he does ghost[1] tours in the town centre. He was 17 when he started and he loves doing it. "I started because I love ghost stories," he says. "There are lots of ghosts in the town because it's so old." The tours aren't expensive: only £5 for adults and £3 for kids. He usually has about 20 people in the group. Is the tour scary? "Yes, of course!" says Jack. "But it's funny too. It's fun for all the family".

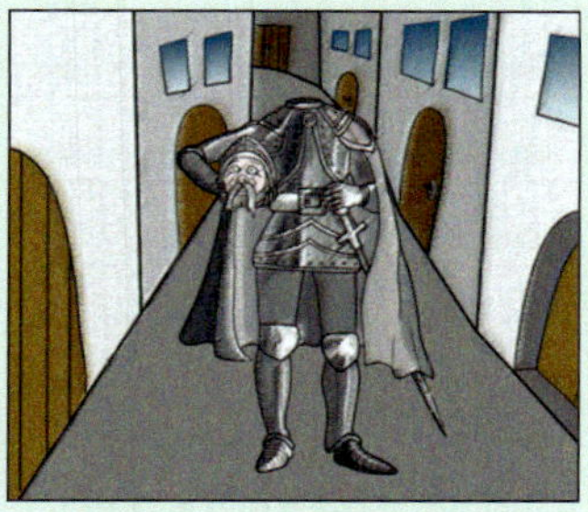

1 What is Jack's hobby? He does ghost tours.

2 When does he do the tours? He does them in the evenings in summer.

3 When did he start? He started when he was 17.

4 What are the tours like? They are scary but funny too.

5 Would you like this hobby? Why (not)? I wouldn't like this hobby because I don't like scary stories!

6 ★ FAST FINISHERS Top 5 strangest hobbies!

Read the article. Choose three of the hobbies and write about them in German for a friend.

You don't have to translate every word.

1 Extreme ironing[2]

Do you think ironing is boring? Try extreme ironing! Do the ironing up a mountain, on water skis, freefall skydiving, at the bottom of the ocean, on a motorbike, on an iceberg …

2 Crocodile bungee jumping

Most people think bungee jumping is scary – but some Aussies don't think it's scary enough. They prefer to bunjee jump into water with crocodiles in it! Are they absolutely crazy?

3 Mooing! (Yes, mooing!)

Can you moo[3] like a real cow? In country towns and villages in America, there are mooing competitions[4]. People come and … well, moo. Some of them wear cow costumes. And the best "moo" wins!

4 Volcano boarding

You've heard of snowboarding. Why not try volcano boarding? Thousands of people do this on the foothills of Nicaragua's Cerro Negro mountain every year. The fastest volcano boarders reach speeds of up to 80 km/h.

5 Dog grooming[5] – with a difference

We all know about dog competitions. But now there are dog grooming[5] competitions: make your dog look like a tiger, a panda, a camel – or even a fairy or an American football player! But what do the dogs think about it all?!

[1] ghost *Gespenst* [2] iron, vb. *bügeln* [3] moo *muhen* [4] competition *Wettbewerb* [5] groom, vb. hier: *stylen*

1 On holiday

a) Write some questions for your British friend, about his/her summer holiday.

1 *(good holiday?)* Did you have a good holiday?

2 *(where?)* Where were you / Where did you go?

3 *(weather?)* What was the weather like?

4 *(activities?)* What (activities) did you do?

5 *(with parents?)* Did you go with your parents?

b) Imagine these are photos of your British friend's summer holiday. Imagine your friend's answers to questions 1–5 from a):

(Yes, thanks, I had a great holiday.

We were in the mountains.

The weather was sunny/good.

We went swimming and we had picnics. I didn't go with my

parents – I went with some friends.)

2 Doing the housework

What chores are Joe and his family going to do this afternoon?

mum	my big sister	my brother	I	the cat

Mum is going to hoover.

My big sister is going to cut the grass.

My brother is going to fill the dishwasher.

I'm going to tidy my room.

The cat is going to sleep in/on the chair!

3 Asking the way: where is the post office?

Look at the picture and complete the sentences.

1 Go *along* Fenn road to the *newsagent's*.

2 *Turn right* at the *traffic lights*.

3 Then *turn left* at the *car park*.

4 The *post office* is next to the *letter box*.

4 Meetings

12 Listen to four dialogues and note the information about the meetings.

	When can the boy and girl meet?	**Where** can they meet?	Activity?	**At what time** are they going to meet?
1	*Sunday afternoon*	*at Daniel's*	*stuff on the Internet*	*2 pm*
2	*Sunday evening*	*at the cinema*	*cinema*	*6.15 pm*
3	*Friday evening*	*post office*	*drink in cafe*	*3.45 pm*
4	*Sunday afternoon*	*at Daniel's*	*eat cake*	*2.30 pm*

5 TV programmes

What do you think about different sorts of TV programmes? Complete the sentences.

1 *interesting* I think *(soaps)* are *more interesting* than documentaries.

2 *funny* I think *(comedies)* are *funnier* than reality shows.

3 *boring* I think *(crime series)* are *more boring* than soaps.

4 *popular* I think *(cartoons)* are the *most popular* programmes in our class.

5 *good* I think *(films)* are the *best* TV programmes.

6 A short letter

Write to Sarah, an English friend. Tell her about last week. Then tell her two things you're going to do next week. Write about 75 words in your exercise book.

Ideas:
Hi Sarah, I hope you're OK.
Last week was busy! On Monday I ...

Feeling good

1 Find the two mystery words

a) Write words 1–9 and find the advice in yellow. ▼

1 If the way you live is healthy, you feel ...
2 Fruit salad and ice cream is a yummy ...
3 "You eat healthy food? That's great! Keep ... up!"
4 Cola and lemonade are ... drinks.
5 There are lots of fun activities – ... your favourite one for the weekend!
6 "I drink ... water – I don't like juice or coffee."
7 "Hands down low – now up ...!"
8 "My ... to you is: do more sport!"
9 "I don't sleep well. I sleep ... than five hours a night."

			▼					
			1 G	O	O	D		
		2 D	E	S	S	E	R	T
		3 I	T					
4 S	U	G	A	R	Y			
	5 P	I	C	K				
6 M	O	S	T	L	Y			
		7 H	I	G	H			
	8 A	D	V	I	C	E		
		9 L	E	S	S			

b) The advice is: get active

c) Make your own word puzzle for a partner on paper:
○ a word snake ● a puzzle like in a).

Start the puzzle with your word in yellow.

► SB p. 69

2 What people say

a) What do adults often say to young people? Write five sentences.

You should You shouldn't	eat drink sleep	be watch	more hours at night junk food too often too many sugary drinks	too much TV more active!

Also use your own ideas!

1 You shouldn't eat junk food too often.
2 You shouldn't drink too many sugary drinks.
3 You should sleep more hours at night.
4 You should be more active!
5 You shouldn't watch too much TV.

b) ● What do young people want to say to many adults? Use your ideas!

1 You should ... (be more active!)
2 You shouldn't ... (tell me what to do!)
3 You ... (shouldn't eat so much at night!)
4 You ... (don't respect me!) and (you should be more friendly to me.)

► SB p. 69

3 A food pyramid

a) Look at the foods and drinks in the pyramid and write the names.

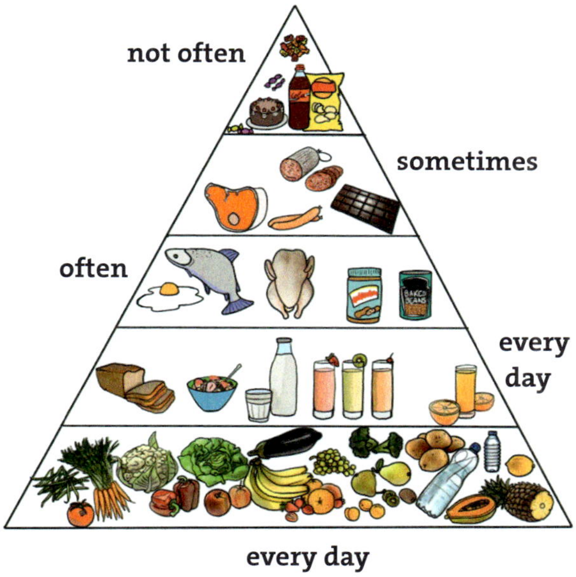

sweets	vegetables
desserts	cola (sugary drinks)
crisps	salami
meat	dark chocolate
fish	peanut butter
chicken	fruit smoothie
eggs	juice
brown bread	water
cereal	salad
milk	fruit

4703

b) Now read the sentences. Are they right (✓) or wrong (✗) according to the pyramid[1]?

1 ✗ It's bad to eat too much salad.
2 ✓ You shouldn't eat too many crisps.
3 ✗ Cola is healthier than milk.
4 ✓ It's important to have some fruit every day.
5 ✓ It's good to eat fish often.
6 ✗ Vegetables are bad for you.

c) Write six "right/wrong" sentences.
Your partner looks at the pyramid and writes ✓ (right) or ✗ (wrong) about your sentences.

Ideas:
- It's good/OK/bad/important | to eat/drink | a lot of ... / quite a lot of ...
- ... is/are bad for you / healthy | ... is/are healthier than ...
- You should have ... every day / often / only sometimes.
- You shouldn't have ... very often.

1 ... ☐
2 ... ☐
3 ... ☐
4 ... ☐
5 ... ☐
6 ... ☐

▸ SB p. 71

[1] according to the pyramid *der Pyramide zufolge*

4 ● Your opinions

Do you think the food pyramid is right? Write what *you* think.

I'm vegetarian. I don't think people should ... | I think people should ... | I don't agree that you should ...

...

...

► SB p. 71

5 ○ Is Ellie ill?

Look again at the dialogue on page 72 of your Student's Book.
Then answer the questions and copy the words in the dialogue that give you the information.

Example: Who says Ellie has missed school before?
Luca He/she says: Ellie isn't at school again today.

1 Who thinks that Ellie says she's ill but maybe she isn't?

Luca He/she says: Do you think she's skiving?

2 Who says they could ask Ellie what's wrong with her?

Mia He/she says: Let's text her and find out.

3 Who knows that Ellie has a problem at home?

Mia He/she says: Her dad has lost his job.

4 Who asks if Ellie's dad is going to live in a new place?

Luca He/she says: Move to a different city?

4805

► SB p. 72

6 ○ Ellie can't work today

a) Write the words 1–8.

1 h a n d
2 l e g
3 a r m
4 h e a d

5 t h r o a t
6 b a c k
7 s t o m a c h
8 k n e e

4806

b) Why can't she work today? Look at the yellow boxes in 6 a) and write a sentence!

Ellie can't work today because she has a headache.

► SB p. 72

7 Your friend doesn't look happy

Write a dialogue between you and your friend.

Be careful with the tenses. Sometimes you'll need the simple past.

hi / how – today?	Hi, there! How are you today ?
terrible! / not – well	Terrible! I'm not feeling well.
☹ / what – matter? / ill? / stomach ache?	Oh dear! What's the matter? Are you ill? Do you have a stomach ache?
headache – really tired	No, I have a headache and I feel really tired.
☹ / what do yesterday?	Poor you! What did you do yesterday?
TV – play on computer – bed late	I watched TV and I played on my computer. I went to bed late.
maybe – should – (...) and (...)	Maybe you should ... and ...

4907

▸ SB p. 73

8 Who's skiving?

Write who is skiving and what's wrong with the five other teens.

1
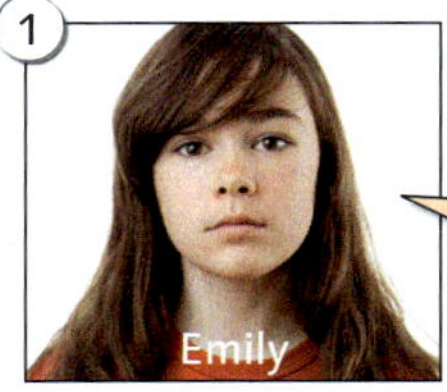

I've eaten five sausages, lots of chips, cake and ice cream.

2

I can't visit Grandma today. I've worked all day and all night. I have to go to bed now!

3

I sing in a group and I sang for ten hours yesterday. Now I can't sing! No school choir for me today!

4

Oh dear – I'm feeling very, very hot.

5
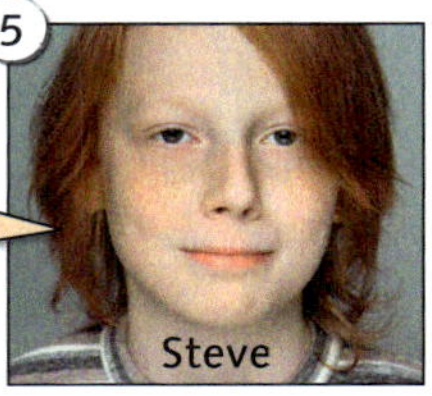

I woke up this morning and I didn't want to go to school.

6
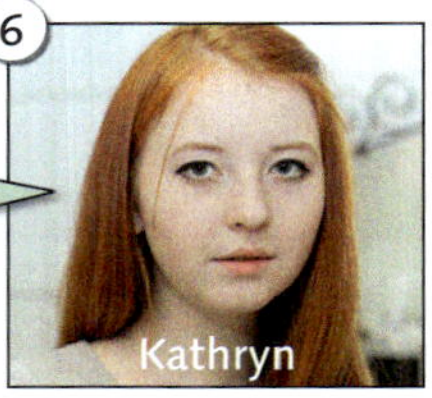

I have a red nose and I sneeze[1] a lot.

Remember:
I have a ...
He/she has a ...

1 Emily has a stomach ache.

2 Iqbal is tired.

3 Dan has a sore throat.

4 Mary has a temperature.

5 Steve is skiving.

6 Kathryn has a cold.

[1] sneeze *niesen*

▸ SB p. 73

9 That's not true!

- Complete the sentences.
- Look at the pictures – is what the people say true (T) or false (F)?

I haven't seen your chocolate! F

(not see)

Sorry, I haven't cooked dinner yet! T

(not cook)

I haven't played football today, Mum! F

(not play)

I haven't forgotten your birthday! T

(not forget)

► SB p. 76

10 A busy house

Look at the picture. What has just happened in this house? Complete the sentences. Use the present perfect.

1 (cook ...) Dan has just cooked dinner.

2 (watch ...) The Taylors have just watched a film.

3 (tidy ...) Megan has just tidied her room.

4 (fill ...) Sue and Kate have just filled the dishwasher.

5010

► SB p. 76

11 What have you done today?

a) Write six questions – put the verbs in the present perfect.

Ideas:
listen / have / see | something beautiful / to the radio / with a good friend
talk / buy / drink | a sugary drink / a maths lesson / something in a shop

See Language file 14 on WB pp. 94–95 for help.

1 Have you listened to the radio today?

2 Have you had a maths lesson?

3 Have you seen something beautiful?

4 Have you talked with a good friend?

b) Now write **three** things you've done today and **three** things you haven't done.

1 I've (had a history lesson) and 2 I've (talked to my friend). 3 I have also (bought something to eat). 4 I haven't (seen my best friend today). 5 I also (haven't watched TV yet). 6 (I haven't helped my mum at home).

5111

c) Now ask your partner questions. Your partner answers *Yes, I have.* or *No, I haven't.*
- questions from a) *"Have you ...?"*
- questions from a) + b) *"I've / I haven't ... Have you?"*

▸ SB p. 76

12 Questions for your favourite music or sports star

a) Write five questions for your favourite star. Use verbs from the box or your own ideas.

verbs with -ed: act • adopt • celebrate • check • chill • clean • collect • cry • help • play • look for • save • ski • visit • vote for • wait for • walk

verbs you must learn: buy • do • drink • eat • have • see

Example: Have you adopted a cat?

My star: name

Have you (celebrated your birthday)?

(Have you saved money)?

Have (you cleaned the kitchen)?

(Have you seen the film ...)?

(Have you cried when ...)?

(Have you seen your parents last month)?

5112

b) Role play. Your partner plays the star. Ask him/her your questions. He/She answers.

▸ SB p. 76

13 Ellie's feelings in the story

Match the beginning and end of the sentences.

1 On Saturday morning Ellie didn't feel like
2 Then she was really disappointed when
3 We know that Ellie was sad because
4 Ellie's mum saw that Ellie was unhappy and
5 Ellie felt a little better when
6 Ellie's friends saw she was different when
7 Ellie was surprised when
8 We know Ellie was happy at the end of the story because

a she ate healthier things at school.
b doing her homework.
c told her she should talk to her dad.
d she smiled more and had fun playing a new sport.
e she talked to her dad.
f her dad told her about his new job.
g she always said No to her friends.
h she found there was no TV in her room.

1 b 2 f 3 g 4 c 5 e 6 a 7 h 8 d

▸ SB p. 79

14 Words from the story

Can you describe more new words on your own? Ask your partner or class to find them.

1 The noise a phone makes – it rings.

2 A person who does technical work is a technician.

3 When a good situation changes to a bad situation, you feel disappointed.

4 A baby cat is a kitten.

5 When you go to someone's house for a few minutes, you stop by.

6 When you go want to see someone, but you can't, you miss them.

7 When you want to change things, but there is nothing you can do, you feel helpless.

8 When you don't want to do something, you don't feel like it.

▸ SB p. 79

15 NOW YOU

Everybody feels sad sometimes. What helps *you* to feel happier again?

a) Write as many ideas as you can.

Example: When I feel sad I text a friend and write: **Let's meet in town.**

When I feel sad I (eat lots of chocolate.) / (... talk to my mum / best friend.)

(... write emails / letters to friends.) / (... play football / a computergame.)

(... sit down and read a book / do homework.)

b) Now look at your partner's ideas and discuss them.

That's a good idea! | I wrote that too. | I never do that! | I should try that!

▸ SB p. 79

16 USING A DICTIONARY Last Sunday

a) Read John's text.
Look at the dictionary entries for the words in blue. Underline the right German words.

Last Sunday I went to a fair. I went with my mates and my little sister Annie came too. The fair was on a large common near our house. First, Annie went on the roundabout (I didn't, of course – it's for kids). Then we had some hotdogs and burgers and my mates and I had a go on the Big Dipper. It was really scary and I felt sick (too many hotdogs!).
The worst moment was when I lost my little sister – panic! I looked and looked, but Annie wasn't there. Then I saw her – she was back on the roundabout again, with a new 'friend'. Phew!!

fair [feə]
1 *n* Jahrmarkt (B)
2 *n* Messe (R)

mate [meɪt]
1 *n* *Zoo.:* Männchen; Weibchen (O)
2 *n* Kumpel (E)

common ['kɒmən]
1 *adj* gewöhnlich (L)
2 *n* Gemeindewiese (N)

roundabout ['raʊndəbaʊt]
1 *n* Kreisverkehr (T)
2 *n* Karussell (J)

kid [kɪd]
1 *n* Kind (A)
2 *v* Spaß machen (U)

sick [sɪk]
1 *someone feels sick* jemandem ist übel (M)
2 *adj* Krank (G)

look [lʊk]
1 *v* aussehen (E)
2 *v* sehen, blicken, gucken (ugs.) (I)

back [bæk]
1 *n* Rücken (P)
2 *adv* zurück (N)

b) Copy the letters next to the right answers in part a) to find the name of Annie's new 'friend'.

BENJAMIN

5316

▸ SB p. 80

17 WRITING A letter

In a *good* letter you can
– give lots of details
– describe your feelings
– say what you think about things.

I'm Anna and I live in a small town in north Spain. I like sunny weather, the sea and swimming. Do you like those things? I'm a music freak too! And I collect stickers and badges – can you send me some? Email is fine, but I like real letters with little presents in them! So who wants to write a real letter to me? I want to know about your life and your country. You can write in English.

a) Read this example snail mail letter. It's very boring and too short!

Dear Anna,

I read your message on the website and I'd like to write you a real letter and send you some stickers!

My name is Maximilian.
I live in Bremen, a town in the north of Germany.
I'm a total music freak too.
My day starts at 6.30 am.
I go to school by bus.
School starts at 8 am.
My favourite lesson is sport.
After school I go to basketball club or I hang out with friends.
I come home at five o'clock.
In the evening I do my homework or watch TV.
I go to bed at 10 o'clock.

Best wishes from Bremen,
...

b) Read the tips. They give you ideas how you can write a more interesting letter.

What do friends call you? Your personality?
My friends say I'm easy going/kind/...

More details?
a big/interesting/old/boring town with lots of good shops/cafes/...

More details?
I love music, especially rap/reggae/...
I sometimes/often go to concerts with ...

What you think about it?
it's too early/terrible/OK/not too bad/...

With ...?
with a good friend/alone/...

Your feelings?
I really like it because I like the teacher / you don't have to sit/. But I don't like maths/... because ...

Where? What do you do?
We sometimes/often/... go to town / read mangas / ...

What do you think about it?
We often have too much / lots of homework. But it's not too bad because ...

How do you feel? So what do you do?
I often feel tired/hungry/fed up, so I ...

5417

c) ○ Write the letter and make it better.
● Write about other things too!

Write in your exercise book or on paper

► SB p. 81

18 PLACEMAT Activities for British students

A group of 18 British students is going to spend a week in your town. What activities could they do?

a) Work in groups of four. Each student takes one colour ( ). My colour: ____________
– First read the dialogue.
– Then write your ideas in the empty boxes – one box for each person.

Take turns!

I've chosen football. I think the British students could watch a big football game in Hamburg.

I agree. Football is cool. Let's take it. → I don't think we should take it. Not everybody likes football. → I agree. And football games are too expensive.

Well, what's your idea?

We could have a barbecue with them. Outdoor activities are fun.

Hm ... But what happens if it rains? → Then we could have the barbecue here at school. → I think it's a nice idea. Then we can talk to the British students. → OK. Let's take it.

What's your idea?

... ____________

... ____________ ... ____________ → ... ____________ ... ____________ → ... ____________ ... ____________

5518

b) Now do the Placemat activity. Draw a placemat on a big piece of paper. Everybody in the group writes three ideas in one corner of the placemat.

c) Read all your ideas.

d) Agree on three activities for the British students. The dialogue in a) can help you. Write them in the middle of your placemat.

e) Tell the class about your ideas. What are the most popular ideas in your group? Say why.

Our first activity is ... We think it's fun/easy/interesting/cheap/...

5519
5520

► SB p. 82

STOP AND PRACTISE

Das habe ich in Unit 4 gelernt:			
Meine Ergebnisse aus **Stop! Check! Go!** im Schülerbuch: ☺ 😐 ☹	Ich kann …	Und wie gut bin ich darin wirklich? ☺ 😐 ☹ Selbsteinschätzung oder Lehrereinschätzung:	Frage deine Lehrerin oder deinen Lehrer nun nach passendem Übungsmaterial.
S. 84 1 ○	1 … über meine Ernährung sprechen und sagen, wie gesund ich lebe. S. 69 – S. 71	○	DFF 4.1 DFF 4.1 DFF 4.1
S. 84 2a ○	2 … Details hören und verstehen. S. 82	○	DFF 4.2 DFF 4.2 DFF 4.2
S. 84 – S. 85 2 ○ 4 ○	3 … über Dinge berichten, die bereits geschehen sind *(present perfect)*. S. 74 – S. 76	○	DFF 4.3 DFF 4.3 DFF 4.3
S. 85 3 ○	4 … sagen, dass ich krank bin und was man dagegen tun kann. S. 72 – S. 73	○	DFF 4.4 DFF 4.4 DFF 4.4
S. 86 6 ○	5 … mich in einer Mail vorstellen und beschreiben. S. 81	○	DFF 4.5 DFF 4.5 DFF 4.5
S. 86 7 ○	6 … ein Poster lesen und verstehen und Auskunft darüber geben. S. 71	○	DFF 4.6 DFF 4.6 DFF 4.6
Diese Fertigkeiten hast du auch geübt. Schätze selbst ein, wie gut du sie schon beherrschst.	7 … sagen, ob viel oder wenig vorhanden ist *(much, many, a lot of, lots of)*. S. 71	○	DFF 4.7 DFF 4.7 DFF 4.7
	8 … jemandem Tipps geben, um sich besser zu fühlen. S. 77 – S. 79	○	DFF 4.8 DFF 4.8 DFF 4.8
	9 … die richtige Wortbedeutung im Wörterbuch erkennen. S. 80	○	DFF 4.9 DFF 4.9 DFF 4.9

Auf diesen Seiten im Schülerbuch findest du die Inhalte.

Auf den folgenden Seiten findest du weitere Übungen, die zu den Lernschwerpunkten passen.

Du kannst diese Seite auch in dein Dossier heften, wenn du fertig bist.

Bitte beachten Sie auf Seite 12 den Hinweis zur Verwendung der Materialien aus „Differenzieren Fördern Fordern“, die sich nach dieser Einschätzung anbietet.

1 Your food pyramid

p. 90

a) What do you eat and drink every week? Write the foods and drinks in your pyramid. Look back at exercise 3 for ideas.

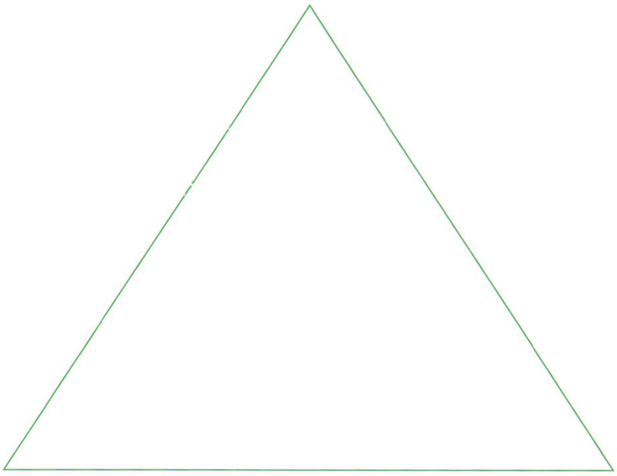

b) Now write three sentences about what you eat and drink.
Use these expressions: *mostly – lots of – too many – not … enough*

1 (I drink lots of water.)

2 (I eat too many potatoes.)

3 (I don't eat enough vegetables.)

► SB p. 70, 71

2 At the doctor's

13

p. 90

a) Listen to four people at the doctor's. Write the picture number for each person:

Mrs Graves: Picture 5,

Mr Robertson: Picture 4,

Miss Abbot: Picture 1,

Mr Jones: Picture 3

1

2

3

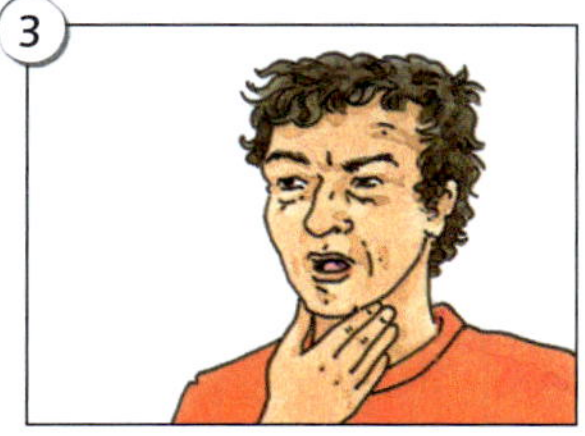

4

5

6

b) Listen again and complete the sentences.

1 **Mrs Graves** hasn't slept well for about two weeks. She's worried because her son has lost his job.

2 **Mr Robertson** has had his problem for two days. The doctor says he should go to the hospital.

3 The doctor tells **Miss Abbot** that she should be in bed. He says that she should drink lots of water or tea.

4 **Mr Jones** has a very sore throat, but he doesn't have a headache.

► SB p. 72, 73

p. 90

3 The Food Doctor

What did the Food Doctor say? Answer the questions in sentences.

1 Which are the healthiest: crisps, nuts or popcorn? Nuts are the healthiest.

2 What sort of chocolate is healthy? Dark chocolate is healthy.

3 Why are smoothies usually good for you? They're good for you because you need lots of fruit.

4 But why are some smoothies not so healthy? They're not so healthy because they have too much sugar.

▸ SB p. 71

p. 91

4 Maths homework

Complete the dialogue with the present perfect form of the verbs. Some are short answers.

Mia — Oh, hi Luca. Have you started *(start)* the maths homework yet?

Luca — No, I haven't, because Grace is here and I've played *(play)* some games with her. Why, what's the matter?

Mia — Well, I've tried *(try)* to do it, but it's too hard!

Luca — I'm sorry I can't help you, Mia. Have you phoned *(phone)* Ellie? Perhaps she's finished *(finish)* her homework.

Mia — No, she hasn't. I know because I've already talked *(talk)* to her!

▸ SB p. 76

p. 91

5 Ellie has decided to change things

What has Ellie done today?
Write the sentences – use the present perfect.

Help mum ✓
Eat a good breakfast ✓
Drink lots of water ✓
Don't buy any crisps ✓
Do my homework ✓
Don't watch TV ✓

Ellie has helped her mum at home. She has eaten a good breakfast and drunk lots of water.

She also hasn't bought any crisps. Ellie has done her homework. Ellie and Zoe haven't watched TV.

So Ellie is feeling happy with herself – and she can eat a nice piece of chocolate cake!

▸ SB p. 76

6 ★ FAST FINISHERS **Problem Page letters**

a) Imagine you work for *Teens* magazine. Read the letters from three readers.

TEENS MAGAZINE

Hi,
I wonder if you can help me? My parents say I don't work enough for school because I like going out with my friends. And now I have a girlfriend – but I haven't told my parents. I know they'll say "You don't have time for girlfriends. School work is more important than having a girlfriend." What should I do?
William

Dear *Teens*,
I have an easy life. I have nice friends and good parents and I find school work OK.
But in the last two weeks I have stopped feeling good about things. I don't feel like working and I don't feel like going out. I don't feel like doing anything! Is something wrong with me? Please help!
Emma

Hi there,
My dad has left our family and my mum is often ill. So I do a lot of work at home because my brothers and sisters are all younger than me. The problem is that I don't have enough time for my school work and some of the teachers are angry with me. Should I tell my mum? Or should I talk to a teacher?
Kevin

b) Answer one of the letters. Write what the person should or shouldn't do.

Hi *(name)* ____________,
Thanks for your letter and thank you for telling me about your problem.

I think ... ______________________________

____

____

____

____

I hope this helps you! Best wishes from *Teens* magazine

c) Reading circle. Look at all the answers. Which answer has the best ideas?

d) Invent[1] another 'problem letter' for *Teens* magazine. Then exchange letters with a partner. Read your partner's letter and say what the writer should or shouldn't do.

Examples:

Hi *Teens*,
there is something I'd like to talk about: My best friend, Michael, is really helpful. But last week he has ...

Dear Bella,
Thanks for your letter.
It's great to have a best friend. But if there's a problem with him or her, it can be hard to talk about it. You should ...

[1] invent *erfinden*

Dartmoor adventures

1 An interview with a ranger in Dartmoor.

a) Answer the questions.

1 What is Dartmoor and where is it?

Dartmoor is a national park in the south west of England.

2 Does it have high mountains?

No, but it has rivers, trees and hills.

3 What animals can you see on Dartmoor?

You can see ponies, sheep, owls, foxes and badgers.

4 Why must you drive carefully on Dartmoor?

Because the sheep walk on the roads.

b) Now write questions for these answers.

5 What (activities) can you do on Dartmoor?
– You can go tree surfing, hang-gliding, mud running and climbing, for example.

6 What are tors?
– They are special hills on Dartmoor.

7 Are there stories about Dartmoor?
– Yes, there are stories like *The Hound of the Baskervilles* and *The Hairy Hands*.

8 Why shouldn't you feed the ponies?
– Because they could bite you!

6001

c) Now find a partner and practise the interview.

► SB p. 89

2 A national park in Germany

Write about a national park or a nice place in Germany.

The text on page 88 in your book can help you!

Useful phrases:
... is a national park in the ... of Germany • It's a ... place with ... • You can see ... • There are lots of ... • It's nice there in (summer). • I go there with ... • People like it because ...

...

...

...

...

► SB p. 89

3 Things for a trip

a) Write words 1–12 and find the two words in yellow. What's this?

1 
2 
3 
4 
5 
6 
7 
8 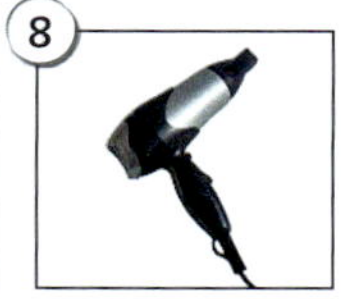
9 
10 
11 
12 

					▼						
		1 S	U	N	C	R	E	A	M		
			2 B	O	O	T	S				
	3 P	Y	J	A	M	A	S				
	4 S	L	E	E	P	I	N	G	B	A	G
				5 R	U	C	K	S	A	C	K
					T	E	N	T			
7 R	A	I	N	G	E	A	R				
8 H	A	I	R	D	R	Y	E	R			
		9 S	U	N	G	L	A	S	S	E	S
			10 T	R	A	I	N	E	R	S	
					M	O	B	I	L	E	
		12 C	A	M	E	R	A				

The words in yellow are: computer game

b) What other things could you take on a trip? Write as many words as you can!

Things that are useful	Things that are fun / nice to have
hat, drinks, (jacket, pen, gloves, camera, socks, food, shirt, paper)	football, (cards, book, mp3 player, guitar, sweets, make-up)

6103

► SB p. 91

4 What do you think?

Which is better – and why?

1 a tent or a dormitory[1]? 2 a trip to Dartmoor or a trip to the sea? 3 an e-reader or a book?

1 I think a ______ is better because ______

2 I think ______

3 ______

► SB p. 91

[1] dormitory ['dɔ:mətri] *Schlafsaal*

5 Camping on Dartmoor.

Look at the picture. Then complete the sentences below it and write two sentences yourself.

1 In the middle I can see *three tents* and *some sleeping bags.*

2 On the right some kids are swimming in *the river.*

3 Between the tent and the river a pony is eating *the kids' food.*

4 The kids on the left are *cooking something to eat.*

5 Behind them there are *some sheep.*

6 The problem is that *there's a black cloud / it will rain.*

▸ SB p. 91

6 The maze game

What do you tell your partner at points 1–6 in the game? Pick the right phrases.

Look at page 92 in your book to find help.

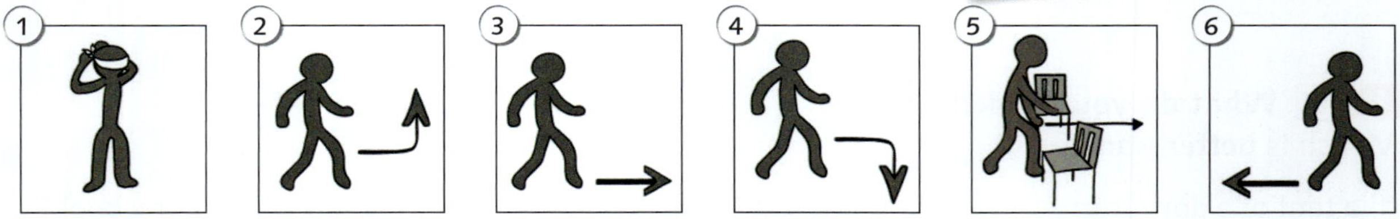

1 *Cover your eyes.*

2 *Turn left.*

3 *Go straight on.*

4 *Turn right.*

5 *There's a chair in front of you / on the left. Walk slowly.*

6 *Go back one step / a bit.*

6206

▸ SB p. 92

7 Going on a trip

a) Write as many words as you can in the networks.

Find ideas on pages 91 and 93 in your book!

You should wear …
- a hoodie
- a jacket
- …
- …
- walking boots
- …

If you need help you should use …
- a mobile
- …
- …
- …
- a whistle
- …

You should take …
- a map
- a plastic bag
- …
- …
- a compass
- …

6307

b) Now look at the two rules below. They're <u>wrong</u>! Write correct rules.

► **If you need help, you should be quiet.**

If you need help, you should shout / make a noise / use a whistle.

► **If you need help, you should leave the group.**

If you need help, you should stay together.

► SB p. 93

8 <u>Your</u> trip to Dartmoor

Imagine[1] you'll walk for two days on Dartmoor next week. You'll sleep in a tent and you'll have to cook in the evening. Your leader wants to know what you'll take and why. Write about five things.

More help p. 86

Example: I'll take a whistle because I can use it if I need help.

1 I'll take a sleeping bag because I don't want to be cold at night.

2 I'll take two bottles of water because I don't want to be thirsty.

3 I'll take my e-reader because I like reading when I go to bed.

4 I'll take my walking boots because they're very comfortable.

5 I'll take crisps because I'm often hungry when I walk.

6308

► SB p. 93

[1] imagine sth. *sich etwas vorstellen*

9 Before the Eggy trip to Dartmoor

Ellie tells her dad about next week's trip.
Write: 'll/won't and pick the right verb[1]:

forget • go • have • meet • sleep • tell

1 We have our trip to Dartmoor next week. I'll go with Mia, Luca and Adam.

2 Our beds are in dormitories, so we won't sleep in a tent.

3 At night, we'll tell lots of scary stories!

4 Miss Lee says we'll have an adventure on Dartmoor on Sunday.

5 I won't forget my rain gear because it often rains there.

6 Luca hopes we won't meet cows because he's scared of them!

6409

► SB p. 95

10 Saturday at the Adventure Centre

14 **a)** What activities will the kids do on Saturday? Listen to the centre leader. Then write the right order of the activities they will do.

A

B

C

D

E

F

G

H

The right order of activities: F, H, D, A, E

b) Now you are the leader at the adventure centre – you choose the activities for today! Tell the students what they will/won't do today.

Choose activities from A–H or others.

...

...

...

...

...

6410

► SB p. 95

[1] verb *Verb*

11 Oh, don't worry, Mum!

a) Daniel is going on a school trip. Write his mum's questions.

1 Where – sleep? *Where will you sleep?*

2 What – eat ? *What will you eat?*

3 be – foggy? *Will it be foggy?*

4 phone – every day? *Will you phone me every day?*

5 Which park – visit? *Which park will you visit?*

6 ranger – go with you? *Will a ranger go with you?*

7 When – trip finish? *When will the trip finish?*

8 activities – be – dangerous? *Will the activities be dangerous?*

6511

b) Write two more questions from Daniel's mum.

Did you check out LF 16 on WB p.95?

...

...

c) Imagine what Daniel says to his mum.

Oh Mum, don't worry so much! ...

► SB p. 95

12 Your plans for the week

You can do any activity you want.

More help p. 87

Imagine: you have a week's holiday. Look at the weather forecast and think about what you'll do.

Example: On Monday it'll be windy, so I'll probably go for a trip on my private boat.

Ideas:
I'll probably[1] ... • I'll maybe ... •
I think I'll ... • ..., so it's the best to ...

Mon  ...

Tues  ...

Wed  ...

Thurs  ...

Fri  ...

► SB p. 96

[1] probably *wahrscheinlich*

13 The story

Put the pictures in the right order for the story (1–8).

► SB p. 99

14 People and feelings

Finish the sentences from the red and blue stories.

1 Nico was embarrassed because (his jacket was on a scarecrow.)

2 Adam was embarrassed because (his clothes were wet.)

3 Mia was frightened because (she saw hairy hands on her food.)

4 The German kids were scared when (they heard a 'hound'.)

5 Luca felt shy when (he said he was the 'hound'.)

6 The two teams were happy when (they walked home together.)

► SB p. 99

6614

15 Directions

Write the right word from the blue story.

The word is a preposition!

1 "Let's go  the village." through

2 "It's on a scarecrow  the village". near

3 The four friends from Eggy walked slowly 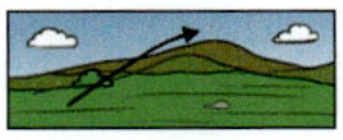 the hill. up

4 The blue team went 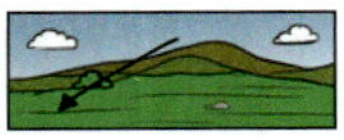 the hill quickly. down

5 Then he slipped and ... SPLASH! ... fell  the river. into

6 The blue team ran  the cottage. out of

7 Ellie ... made a tent  the rocks. between

8 Everybody walked back  Green Road. along

► SB p. 99

16 READING Man's best friend

a) Look at the heading and the photo. What do you think the text is about?

1 ☐ a rescue group 2 ☐ how you can train[1] your pet 3 ☑ how dogs learn to rescue people

b) Read the text and check your answer.

Rescue Dog Training

Training to be a rescue dog starts when the dog is about six months. A dog has a very sensitive nose! When the dog finds a person by scent and shows its handler where the person is, it gets a reward.
The dog soon learns to find the person quickly. But it has to learn to ignore other things, for example sheep and cows. They can make the dog forget what it's doing. It also has to be able to work when the weather is very bad. When the dog is ready, it has a test – is it good enough to join the team? It's a test for the handler, too – can he or she work well with the dog? If the dog passes the test, everyone is happy!

c) Find and underline these four important words in the text: scent – handler – ignore – pass
Think: what do you think they mean in German? Then check at the bottom of this page.

d) Now answer these questions.

1 How old is a dog when it starts training? *It's six months.*

2 How does it find missing people? *It smells them.*

3 Why are other animals sometimes a problem? *They can make the dog forget what it's doing.*

4 When can the dog join the team? *When it passes / is good at a test.*

► SB p. 100

17 LISTENING Police, fire or ambulance?

15

Listen and complete the forms[2].

Police ☑	Fire ☐	Ambulance ☐
Name	*Archer*	
Phone number	*077 382 217 029*	
Where?	*Union Street / Martin Street*	
Number of people	*5*	

Police ☐	Fire ☐	Ambulance ☑
Name	*Johnson*	
Phone number	*078 437 972 486*	
Where?	*Hoe park, near Lighthouse*	
Number of people	*2*	

6717

► SB p. 100

[1] train, vb. *trainieren* [2] forms *Formulare*

scent *Geruch* (dog) handler *Hundetrainer/-in, Hundeführer/-in* ignore *ignorieren* pass a test *bestehen*

18 SPEAKING An accident

a) A German family on holiday in England have had an accident in their car. They phone the police. Complete the dialogue.

Assistant __ Hello. Which service do you need – ambulance, fire or police?

Julian __ Police please.

Assistant __ What has happened?

Julian __ We've had an accident.

Assistant __ OK. What are your name and your phone number, please?

Julian __ Julian Förster. 00 49 176 6395.

Assistant __ OK. And where are you?

Julian __ We're on the road from Gunnislake to Plymouth, about 2 miles from Plymouth.

Assistant __ Is anybody hurt?

Julian __ No. Everybody is OK.

Assistant __ OK, thank you. The police will be there ______ in twenty minutes.

6818

b) Read the dialogue with your partner.

► SB p. 101

19 WRITING Picture Story

Write what the people say.

1: need help – friend / accident – Dartmoor

2: OK? – happen? – hurt?

3: foggy – fall – hurt / leg

1 (Hello. We need help. My friend has had an accident. We're on Dartmoor.)

2 (Are you OK? What (has) happened? Are you hurt?)

3 (It was foggy and I fell. I've hurt my leg.)

► SB p. 101

20 CORRECTING A letter from Hannah

Read the letter from Hannah to her friends in Plymouth. Find and mark the mistakes.

1 Sentences should start with a capital letter.
• Correct 5 mistakes.

2 Some words need capitals (e.g. names, days, months). But most don't need them.
• Correct 7 mistakes.

3 'I' always needs a capital letter.
• Correct 3 mistakes.

4 With time phrases like 'last Friday' or 'yesterday', you need the simple past.
• Correct 5 mistakes.

5 Is the sentence about the future (tomorrow/ next week)? Then you need 'will' (or 'll).
• Correct 3 mistakes.

Dear Ellie, Luca, Adam and Mia,

hi. I hope You're all well. I'm happy because my Leg is now much better again. last Tuesday i go to the Doctor. She say my leg is fine. It doesn't hurt now. Yesterday we have a party at Nico's house. it was fun. Alex bring some English sausages! He had them from Plymouth and We all think of you when we ate them! but I'm sorry, i think German sausages are better ! ☺ We have no School tomorrow, so I think i go to Town. I want to buy some new Clothes and I hope I find some nice things. ☺ after that I go to Nico's House.

Love Hannah

6920

► SB p. 102

21 WRITING Your email

a) Write an email to an English friend.
Write as many sentences as you can.
Tell him or her
- how you feel
- what you did yesterday or last weekend
- your plans for tomorrow or next weekend.

If you can, write your email on a computer. It's easier to correct.

6922
6923

b) Show your email to a partner. Read and correct your partner's email.

c) Then write your letter on a different sheet of paper. Put it in your dossier.

► SB p. 102

STOP AND PRACTISE

Das habe ich in Unit 5 gelernt:			
Meine Ergebnisse aus Stop! Check! Go! im Schülerbuch: ☺ 😐 ☹	Ich kann …	Und wie gut bin ich darin wirklich? ☺ 😐 ☹ Selbsteinschätzung oder Lehrereinschätzung:	Frage deine Lehrerin oder deinen Lehrer nun nach passendem Übungsmaterial.
S. 104 2 ◯	1 … sagen, welche Ausrüstung man für einen Ausflug braucht. S. 90 – S. 91, S. 93	◯	DFF 5.1 DFF 5.1 DFF 5.1
S. 105 3 ◯	2 … Aussagen über das Wetter machen. S. 96	◯	DFF 5.2 DFF 5.2 DFF 5.2
S. 105 4 ◯	3 … sagen, auf welche Art und Weise etwas getan wird *(adverbs)*. S. 92 – S. 93	◯	DFF 5.3 DFF 5.3 DFF 5.3
S. 106 – S. 107 5 ◯ 7 ◯	4 … Aussagen darüber machen, was in der Zukunft passieren oder nicht passieren wird *(will/won't)*. S. 94 – S. 96	◯	DFF 5.4 DFF 5.4 DFF 5.4
S. 106 6a ◯	5 … typische Fehler in einem englischen Text erkennen und korrigieren. S. 102	◯	DFF 5.5 DFF 5.5 DFF 5.5
S. 106 6b ◯	6 … eine Postkarte schreiben. S. 102	◯	DFF 5.6 DFF 5.6 DFF 5.6
Diese Fertigkeiten hast du auch geübt. Schätze selbst ein, wie gut du sie schon beherrschst.	7 … einen Text über Dartmoor lesen und ihm Informationen entnehmen. S. 88 – S. 89	◯	DFF 5.7 DFF 5.7 DFF 5.7
	8 … Durchsagen an einem Bahnhof verstehen und Informationen auf Deutsch weitergeben. S. 100	◯	DFF 5.8 DFF 5.8 DFF 5.8
	9 … bei der Notrufzentrale anrufen. S. 100 – S. 101	◯	DFF 5.9 DFF 5.9 DFF 5.9

Auf diesen Seiten im Schülerbuch findest du die Inhalte.

Auf den folgenden Seiten findest du weitere Übungen, die zu den Lernschwerpunkten passen.

Du kannst diese Seite auch in dein Dossier heften, wenn du fertig bist.

Bitte beachten Sie auf Seite 12 den Hinweis zur Verwendung der Materialien aus „Differenzieren Fördern Fordern", die sich nach dieser Einschätzung anbietet.

p. 91

1 A camping trip

a) Look at the picture. What did the kids take with them? How many things can you find in two minutes?

6–9: good 10–12: very good more than 12: excellent[1]!

trainers	sun cream
tent	map
sunglasses	sweets
boots	compass
sleeping bag	first aid kit
rucksack	whistle
mobile	plastic bag

b) Look at the picture again. Then answer the questions.

Will the kids go hang-gliding tomorrow? What will they do?

No, they won't (go hang-gliding). They'll go climbing and mud running.

c) Imagine you're on a camping trip. Write a postcard to your English friend Catherine.

Tell her:

- where you are and what the weather is like
- what you **did** yesterday and say why it was fun!
- what you**'re doing** today
- what you think the weather **will be** like tomorrow
- what you**'ll** probably **do**
- what you hope **won't** happen tomorrow (and why!).

Dear Catherine,

(I'm camping with some friends on Dartmoor.
The weather is good! Yesterday we went walking.
It was fun because our teacher fell into the river.
Today we're going hang-gliding. I think it'll be
sunny tomorrow and we'll probably go climbing.
I hope we won't climb very high because I don't
like to look down!
Best wishes
...)

▸ SB p. 91, 93

[1] excellent *ausgezeichnet*

p. 91

16

2 The weather forecast

a) Five things are WRONG on this weather map (symbols[1] or temperature). Listen to the weather forecast.

- Draw correct symbols
- Write the correct temperature

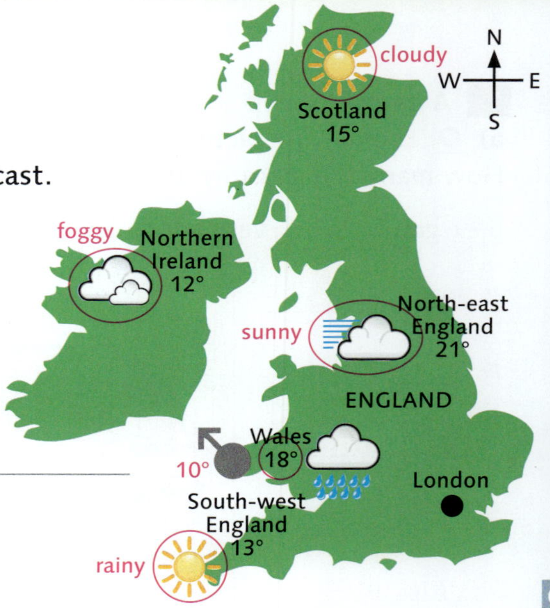

Northern Ireland *Nordirland*

b) Listen again. Then write notes.

1 What will the weather be like in Wales today?

rainy and windy, temperature – 10 degrees

2 Will the weather be better at the weekend? What will it be like?

no – foggy and cloudy

► SB p. 96

p. 91

3 Adjective or adverb?

Read the sentences. Choose and write the right answer: a or b.

Look at the rules on page 186 in your book.

1 Ellie is good at sport. She can run quickly. a) *quick* b) *quickly*

2 Her mum often says she's often noisy at home. a) *noisy* b) *noisily*

3 And when she laughs, she laughs happily. a) *happy* b) *happily*

4 Her teachers say that she works slowly. a) *slow* b) *slowly*

5 But she says that she is very careful with her work. a) *careful* b) *carefully*

6 She has good friends and is popular in her class. a) *popular* b) *popularly*

► SB p. 70, 71

p. 92

4 What do you think will happen?

Complete these sentences.

1 Mark sees a black cloud. I think he'll put on his rain gear.

2 Some people are having a picnic. I think they'll leave their litter.

3 I think Mark will pick up the litter – or the ponies will eat it.

► SB p. 76

[1] symbols *Symbole*

5 ★ FAST FINISHERS A day on Dartmoor

Mrs Burton and her children went walking on Dartmoor.
Choose a good order for the pictures and write a story.

walk ▸ walked
drive ▸ drove

p. 92

ambulance men

walk – boots – rain

fall – shout – hurt

walk again – bridge

tired – picnic

phone – sit – leg

drive – sheep – tor

your picture!

8

Four days later ...

Start like this: *One Saturday afternoon Mrs Burton and her two children drove across ...*

6 ★ FAST FINISHERS A quiz about Dartmoor

You're going to make a quiz about Dartmoor for friends in the class.

Useful question words:
where / what / why / when / who /
how far / how much / how many

- Work with a partner or in a small group.
- Find information about Dartmoor:
  – in the student's book /
  – on the internet /
  – in a book or brochure / ...

- Choose what type(s) of question you'll use:

  True or False?
  Dartmoor has a famous castle. *True* ☐ / *False* ☐

  Answer the questions. *What is a tor?* ______

  Tick (✔) the right answer.
  Dartmoor is in the
  a) ☐ *south-west* *b)* ☐ *south-east* *c)* ☐ *north-west*

- Write your questions.
  Can you write them on a computer?
  Don't forget to write the answers – you'll need them!

- Check your questions – and correct any mistakes.

- Can you find some pictures of Dartmoor? Your quiz will look better!

- Write or print your quiz.

- Give the quiz to friends in the class.

Who gets the most right answers?

A journey in time

1 A quiz about Arthur, Francis Drake and the Pilgrims

a) First look at the six pictures below and write the words.

A S W O R D B C O A S T C S H I P

D S A I L O R E K I N G F M A G I C I A N

b) Now read the sentences below. Pick the right answer and follow the arrow (→) to the next box. Then pick the right answer again.
If you choose the right answers, the red letters give you the name of Arthur's sword.

1 Arthur pulled a

A

from ...

the sea **N**	a stone **E**
→ 4	→ 5

2 The Pilgrims also left from this

B

They sailed for ...

16 days **F**	66 days **B**
→ 6	→ 3

3 Their

C

was the ...

Merlin **O**	Mayflower **U**
→ 5	→ 9

4 Later Francis Drake was a

D

here. He lived near ...

London **E**	Plymouth **A**
→ 2	→ 8

5 He became

E

of ...

England **X**	Scotland **R**
→ 7	→ 9

6 In 1588 he fought against the Spanish ...

Armada **I**	smugglers **O**
→ 2	→ 9

7 A

F

helped Arthur. His name was ...

Merlin **C**	Mayflower **D**
→ 4	→ 5

8 In 1577 Drake sailed round the world.

For this Drake was very ...

big **V**	famous **L**
→ 7	→ 6

9 The Pilgrims started a new life in North ...

Africa **M**	America **R**

7401

▶ The name of Arthur's sword was EXCALIBUR.

▸ SB p. 109

2 Two sentences – one meaning

Sentence B) means the same as sentence A).
Find the right words to complete sentence B).

1 **A** After a long time, the new museum opened on Tuesday.
= **B** The new museum *finally* ______ opened on Tuesday.

2 **A** It has information about lots of different themes.
= **B** It has information about lots of different *topics* ______.

You can find all the words on pages 110 and 111 in your book.

3 **A** You can learn about lots of things that happened in the past.
= **B** You can learn about lots of *historic* ______ *events* ______.

4 **A** History feels real at this museum. = **B** History *comes* ______ *alive* ______ at this museum.

5 **A** There's a tour every day. = **B** There's a *daily* ______ tour.

6 **A** Your museum ticket gives you a free trip on the river.
= **B** Your museum ticket gives you a free *boat* ______ trip.

7 **A** I don't think that's true! = **B** I don't *believe* ______ that!

8 **A** It is true. I know the boss of the boat. = **B** It is true. I know the *captain* ______ of the boat.

7502

▸ SB p. 111

3 What will you do tomorrow?

a) Write what Daniel could say.

Example: *If it's good weather, I'll go out.*

1 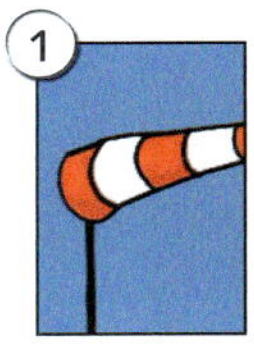
2 
3 
4 

... go for a walk. 
... do some chores. 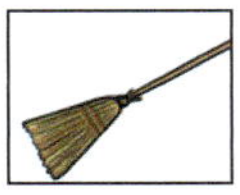
... make a snowman! 
... go sailing. 

1 *If it's windy, I'll go sailing.*
2 *If it's sunny, I'll go for a walk.*
3 *If it's rainy, I'll do some chores.*
4 *If it's snowy, I'll make a snowman!*

b) What will or won't you do tomorrow?
Write three sentences.

If you need help, look at the Language File 17 on page 187 in your book!

1 If it's ______________, I'll ______________
2 If ______________
3 ______________

7503

▸ SB p. 111

4 What happens in the story?

Story "we ..." "our mobiles ..." ▶ **Your answer** "they ..." ▶ "their mobiles ..." etc.

a) *Scenes 1 & 2* Answer the questions – the information is in the story.

1 Why doesn't Luca like the tour? *He thinks it's a bit long.*

2 It's dark on the stairs. How do the friends see? *They use the light from their mobiles.*

3 Why does Arthur need their help? *He's lost / He has to get back to Tintagel.*

4 Why is it difficult for the friends to help him? *They're lost too.*

▶ SB p. 112

b) *Scenes 3 & 4* True or False?

	True	False
1 Rover is William's dog.		✓
2 The Mayflower was before the Spanish Armada.		✓
3 John plays the drum for Sir Francis Drake.	✓	
4 Merlin sent Arthur to Plymouth by mistake.		✓
5 The history kids will go back when it gets dark.	✓	
6 The history kids wear the modern kids' jackets because their clothes look strange.	✓	

▶ SB p. 113

c) *Scenes 4 & 5* What four modern things do the history kids find amazing?

bus ____ *lights* ____ *mobile phone* ____ *laptop/computer*

▶ SB p. 114

d) *Scenes 6 & 7* Read the answers – then complete the questions!

1 *Did* Luca *make* the pizza? – No, it's from dinner last night.

2 *When can* Luca's dad *take* the kids to Tintagel? – He can take them there tomorrow.

3 *Who* is *sending* Arthur a *message*? – Merlin is sending him a message.

4 *Where* must William and Mary *stand*? – On the Mayflower steps.

5 *Why do* they *go* to the Hoe? – Because there's a statue of Sir Francis there.

▶ SB p. 116

e) *Scene 8* The history kids want to go home – what do they have to do?

They all *have to hold hands.*

Arthur *has to say/remember a magic rhyme.*

▶ SB p. 117

Do you see the information boxes on pages 114 and 115 in your book?

5 Numbers in the story

Look at the information Luca finds on his laptop. Write sentences with these numbers.

1 *1620/06/09/11/11* In 1620, the Mayflower sailed from Plymouth on 6th September and arrived in North America on 11th November.

2 *132/1588/67* 132 Spanish ships sailed to England in 1588. Only 67 came back to Spain.

3 *46* Tintagel is 46 miles from Plymouth.

▸ *SB p. 115*

6 The story: which version is right?

Which is right? Tick (✓) A, B or C.

A ☐ Our friends have got lost in the past, but some kids tell them some magic rhymes. The rhymes help our kids to come home to Plymouth.

B ☑ Our friends meet some kids from the past who are lost in the present. Our friends and Merlin's magic rhymes finally help the history kids to go home.

C ☐ Some kids from the past are lost in the present. Our friends try to help them, but the history kids can't get home. They have to stay in Plymouth.

▸ *SB p. 117*

7 New words in the story

Find the words in the story and complete the crossword.

Across ➜

2 This word means "stupid". *(scene 7)*
4 A long trip is a ... *(scene 2)*
6 In Plymouth you can buy postcards with a ... of the sea. *(scene 7)*
7 This word means "started". *(scene 5)*
10 Cars, buses and trains are forms of ... *(scene 6)*
11 A magician does this. *(scene 5)*
13 If you didn't see something or didn't hear something, you ... it. *(scene 1)*
14 When it's dark you ... on the lights. *(scene 5)*

Down ⬇

1 This word means "happy". *(scene 1)*
2 Look up and you'll see this! It could be blue. *(scene 3)*
3 This is an animal that people ride. *(scene 4)*
5 You need this to see in the dark. *(scene 1)*
8 The history kids think Luca's laptop is ... *(scene 5)*
9 When my maths homework is too difficult, my dad ... it to me. *(scene 3)*
12 Arthur and Merlin lived a long time ... *(scene 2)*

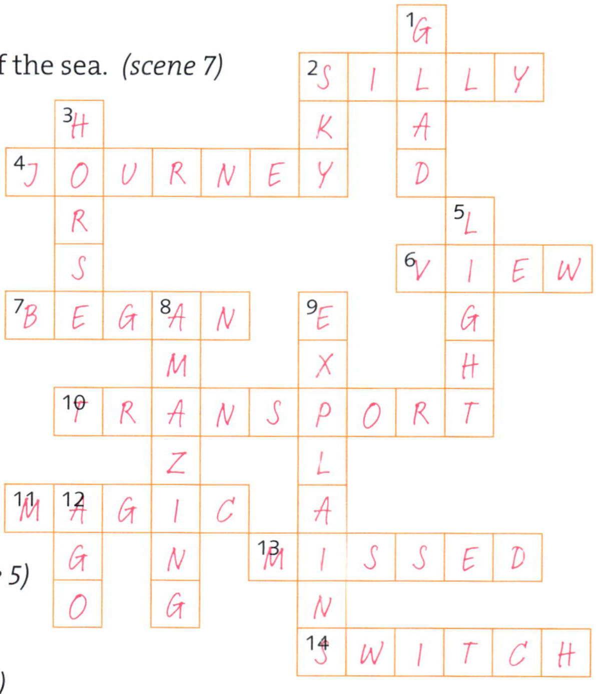

7707

▸ *SB p. 117*

8 LISTENING Choosing a topic for a poster

More help p. 87

17

Four students are trying to choose a topic.

a) Listen to the students and write notes in the table.

Topics	Why?	Why not?
The Romans in Britain	amazing (built lots of things)	did that in history (2 years ago)
Smugglers on Britain's south coast	more exciting	don't have enough information
The Pilgrims	interesting (it's about the history of the USA too)	really boring
King Arthur	has magic and legends	not favourite topic

b) Which topic do they choose? King Arthur

And which topic would you choose? Why?

► SB p. 118

7808

9 CORRECTING Texts for a poster

Two German students have written texts for their posters.
There are four mistakes in each text. Find and correct the mistakes.

A A lot of People say that King Arthur didn't died. They say that at the moment, King Arthur sleeping. They say that if there is real danger in Britain in the future, he come back.

people
die
is sleeping
he'll / he will

built
example
comes
their

B The Romans build many towns in Britain and some are still there today, for Example London, York and Chester. In these cities, you can still see Roman ruins. Roman history come alive in her museums.

► SB p. 119

7809

10 SPEAKING After the gallery walk: can you remember?

Work with a partner. Choose a topic from another group's poster.
Talk about the poster after you've looked at it. How many things can you remember?

So, what did the poster say about The Pilgrims?

Well, their ship was called the Mayflower. That's one thing I can remember.

Yes, and they were Protestants. That's two ...

► SB p. 119

11 What were you doing?

Mr Smith's motorbike[1] is missing. A policeman is asking questions.

a) Complete the sentences. Use the past progressive.

> write ▶ writing (& smile, ride, take)
> run ▶ running

Policeman — Mrs Brown, you live next door to Mr Smith, don't you.

What *were* you *doing* *(do)* yesterday afternoon at about 5pm?

Mrs Brown — I *was tidying* *(tidy)* some things in the garden. Then I suddenly saw two men. They *were standing* *(stand)* near Mr Smith's motorbike. One man *was writing* *(write)* something in a notebook[2]. I think he *was smiling* *(smile)* The other man *was holding* *(hold)* a camera. Ah, here's my son[3], James! Tell the policeman what you *were doing* *(do)* at 5pm.

James — Well, I *was playing* *(play)* with a friend. We *were running* *(run)* along the road.

Policeman — And did you see the motorbike?

James — Yes, a young man *was riding* *(ride)* it. I think he *was wearing* *(wear)* jeans and a red T-shirt.

Mrs Brown — That's one of the men I saw – I'm sure!

> Do you need help? Look at the rules in your book at page 187 (LF 18).

b) What were these other people doing at 5pm?

1 

(Angela was playing basketball.)

2 

(Mr Smith was sleeping.)

3 

(The Wilsons were eating dinner.)

4 

(Sally was doing her homework.)

5 

(Josh was washing the car.)

6 

(Mrs Johns was driving her car.)

7911
7912

▸ SB p. 120

[1] motorbike *Motorrad* [2] notebook *Notizbuch* [3] son *Sohn*

Das habe ich in Unit 6 gelernt:			
Meine Ergebnisse aus **Stop! Check! Go!** im Schülerbuch: ☺ 😐 ☹	Ich kann …	Und wie gut bin ich darin wirklich? ☺ 😐 ☹ Selbsteinschätzung oder Lehrereinschätzung:	Frage deine Lehrerin oder deinen Lehrer nun nach passendem Übungsmaterial.
S. 122 **2** ◯	**1** … Aussagen über bestimmte Bedingungen treffen *(Conditional sentences type 1).* S. 110	◯	DFF 6.1 ⚀ DFF 6.1 ⚁ DFF 6.1 ⚂
S. 122 **3** ◯	**2** … über Handlungen sprechen, die in der Vergangenheit gerade im Gange waren *(past progressive).* S. 120	◯	DFF 6.2 ⚀ DFF 6.2 ⚁ DFF 6.2 ⚂
S. 122 **5** ◯	**3** … ein historisches Ereignis nacherzählen. S. 112 – S. 117	◯	DFF 6.3 ⚀ DFF 6.3 ⚁ DFF 6.3 ⚂
	4 … historische Informationen verstehen und zeitlich einordnen. S. 108 – S. 109	◯	DFF 6.4 ⚀ DFF 6.4 ⚁ DFF 6.4 ⚂
	5 … meine Meinung äußern und mich mit anderen einigen. S. 111	◯	DFF 6.5 ⚀ DFF 6.5 ⚁ DFF 6.5 ⚂
Diese Fertigkeiten hast du auch geübt. Schätze selbst ein, wie gut du sie schon beherrschst.	**6** … ein Hörspiel verstehen. S. 112 – S. 117	◯	DFF 6.6 ⚀ DFF 6.6 ⚁ DFF 6.6 ⚂
	7 … einfache Sachtexte über historische Ereignisse verstehen. S. 114 – S. 115	◯	DFF 6.7 ⚀ DFF 6.7 ⚁ DFF 6.7 ⚂
	8 … ein Thema recherchieren und auf einem Poster präsentieren. S. 118 – S. 119	◯	DFF 6.8 ⚀ DFF 6.8 ⚁ DFF 6.8 ⚂

Auf diesen Seiten im Schülerbuch findest du die Inhalte.

Auf den folgenden Seiten findest du weitere Übungen, die zu den Lernschwerpunkten passen.

Du kannst diese Seite auch in dein Dossier heften, wenn du fertig bist.

Bitte beachten Sie auf Seite 12 den Hinweis zur Verwendung der Materialien aus „Differenzieren Fördern Fordern", die sich nach dieser Einschätzung anbietet.

1 English history

Complete the information with the missing words.

all over • attack • became • built • cave • destroyed • famous • fought • magician • Protestants • ruins • sailed • ship • sword • their own

1 **The Romans** wanted to make Britain their own. They had camps all over the country, but they didn't come to Plymouth.

2 Young **Arthur** pulled a sword from a stone and became king of England. You can still see the ruins of Tintagel Castle, where he lived. Merlin was a magician who helped King Arthur. He lived in a cave near Tintagel.

3 **Francis Drake** was a famous sailor. In July 1588, he was playing bowls in Plymouth when he heard that the Spanish Armada was trying to attack England. Did he panic[1]? No. He finished his game, then went and fought against the Spanish. He destroyed their ships in only eight days.

4 **The Pilgrims** were Protestants who had a hard life in England. In 1620, they sailed from Plymouth in their ship, *The Mayflower*. They built a new town in America – and called it Plymouth!

2 What if …?

What will Nils do in the holidays? Write a sentence for each phrase.

1 have enough money? If I have enough money, I'll go to England.

2 my friend – free? If my friend is free, he'll come with me.

3 be near Plymouth? If we're near Plymouth, we'll visit Tintagel Castle.

4 take our tents? If we take our tents, we'll go camping.

b) And you?

___

[1] panic (vb.) *in Panik ausbrechen*

p. 92

3 ★ FAST FINISHERS Jake's adventure at Tintagel

a) Look at the pictures. Tell Jake's story. Write at least two sentences for each picture.

1

2

3

a wave *eine Welle*

4

5

6

1 Last weekend *Jake and his mum* (went by car to Tintagel. The sun was shining.)

2 (They visited the castle. Jake wasn't interested. He left his mum.)

3 (Jake went down to the sea. There were lots of rocks there. The waves were a bit scary.)

4 (Suddenly a big wave took Jake into the sea. "Help! Help!" he shouted.)

5 (And suddenly he saw Arthur and Merlin. And they helped him out of the water!)

6 (Then Jake's mum came with the police. But Arthur and Merlin weren't there.)

b) Imagine you are Jake. Will you tell your mum and the police about Merlin and Arthur? Why (not)? Write what you'll do.

I'll tell / I won't tell ... because ...

I won't tell my mum and the police about Arthur and Merlin because they'll think I'm crazy / they won't believe me / ...

1 Being healthy

a) Write a food or drink for as many letters of the alphabet as you can!
12–16: good   more than 16: very good!

Apple, bread, carrot, dessert, egg, fruit, goat's milk, hamburger, ice cream, jam,
ketchup, lasagne, meat, nut, orange, potato, rabbit, smoothie, tea, vegetables,
water, yogurt,
zucchini

b) What should you do and what shouldn't you do to be healthy? Write two things for each.

You should ... __________

____

____

c) Now write four things you've eaten and drunk today.

I've ... __________

____

2 At the doctor's

18

a) Listen to three dialogues. Match the pictures with the dialogues.

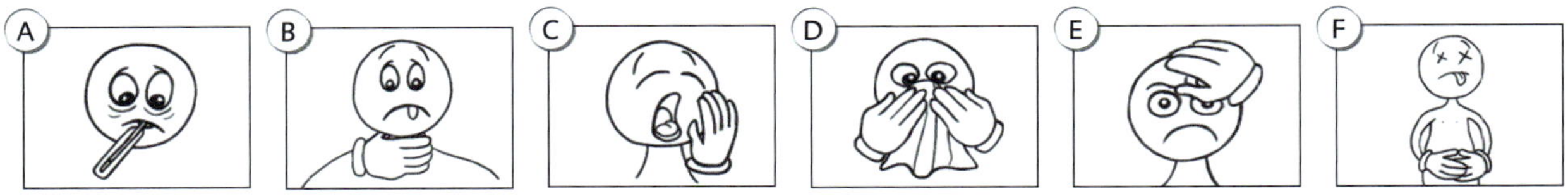

Dialogue 1: *A, D*   Dialogue 2: *C, E*   Dialogue 3: *B, F*

b) Listen again. Answer the questions. Write notes.

1 What should Mrs Thomas do when she is better?

go outside more and *eat healthier food*.

2 Why doesn't Mick sleep well?

He lost his job and *he's worried*.

3 What's the real problem with Charlotte?

She's skiving because *maths is hard/difficult*.

3 A camping trip

a) Imagine you'll go on a camping trip next weekend. Answer the questions.

1 What will you take with you? Write five things and say why you'll take them.

Example: I'll take my camera so I can take lots of photos. I'll take ... because ...

I'll (take a tent because we won't stay in a centre. I'll take a map and a compass so I won't get lost. I'll take rain gear because it could be rainy. I'll take my mobile so I can phone my parents.)

2 What won't you take with you? Write two things.

I (won't take a hair dryer or an e-reader.)

b) Look at the weather forecast and write what the weather will be like next weekend.

Saturday morning

Saturday afternoon

Sunday morning

Sunday afternoon

On Saturday morning it'll be foggy and rainy, but in the afternoon it'll be sunny.

On Sunday morning it'll be windy. In the afternoon it'll be cloudy, but hot.

4 Accident!

Write the verbs to complete the story.
Use the simple past and the past progressive *(was ...ing)*.

Last weekend I *(go)* went into the country with my friend Akbar. We *(ride)* were riding our bikes along a country road when suddenly a car *(come)* came up very fast. A man *(drive)* was driving it and he *(not see)* didn't see us because he *(text)* was texting. The car *(drive)* drove very close to us and Akbar *(fall off)* fell off his bike. I *(shout)* shouted to the man, but he *(not hear)* didn't hear – he *(go)* was going too fast and he *(listen)* was listening to loud music. Luckily, Akbar was OK – but his bike wasn't! We *(have to)* had to walk home.

5 You have won £10,000!

Write an email to your English friend James about your plans for the next holiday.
Write about 60 words in your exercise book.

> Hi James,
> I have great news: I've won £10,000!
> I think I'll ... and I hope ...
> I hope I won't ...!

Unit 1

21 WORDS The rules at your school

Write some ideal or crazy rules for your school! Use: have to / can / mustn't.

You can use these ideas:

Students Teachers You	have to can mustn't	have lots of piercings • wear lots of make-up • have barbecues at break • sing • wear sunglasses • bring their pets to school • give everybody cakes • be too strict • sit next to their friends • use a mobile • listen to music • play cards • skateboard ... in class

1 *Students' own answers*

2 *Students' own answers*

3 *Students' own answers*

4 *Students' own answers*

▸ WB p. 11

Unit 3

2 What did Ellie do at the weekend?

Write sentences.

✓ = she did this
✗ = she didn't do this

She	did / didn't do listened to / didn't listen to met / didn't meet went / didn't go	chores friends music stuff on the computer swimming to the shops	... 10 am ... afternoon before ... after ... ... Sunday ... weekend ... evening

1 ✓  *She went shopping / to the shops at 10 am..*

2 ✓  *She listened to music in the afternoon.*

3 ✓  *She did chores before dinner.*

4 ✗  *She didn't go swimming on Sunday.*

5 ✗  *She didn't meet friends at the weekend.*

6 ✗  *She didn't do stuff on the internet/computer after lunch.*

▸ WB p. 30

5 Teens and money

b) Now write about the results[1]. You can use this text to help you.

You can put your text in your dossier.

A money survey in our class

I talked to 10 students in our class. Five students get pocket money. One student has a job. Four students do chores at home. Three students need money for the cinema. Two students buy clothes. One student buys lots of sweets and chocolate. Four students buy books or comics. All students need money for their mobiles.

► WB p. 32

15 WRITING An email about a hobby

b) Now write your email.

Here are some ideas for your email:

I have a good hobby.

I sing	– in a group / in a choir ...
I play the violin / guitar ...	– in an orchestra / in a band ...
I play handball ...	– in the school team ...
I make	– clothes / toys / models / cakes ...
I do	– judo / gymnastics / stuff on the computer ...
I go	– swimming / riding / skiing / walking ...
I write	– stories / songs / TV scripts ...
I go to	– a drama club / an art club / a computer club
I (...)	– every day / on Tuesdays / at the weekend / after school – in the country / in the town centre / – at school / at the sports centre.
I do it	– with my friends / with people from school / with my step-dad
I like my hobby because	– it's interesting / fun / exciting – I love sport / music / the country

► WB p. 37

Unit 5

8 Your trip to Dartmoor

Imagine you'll walk for two days on Dartmoor next week. You'll sleep in a tent, you'll have to cook in the evening. Your leader wants to know what you'll take and why. Write about five things.

Ideas:
I'll take ... because
... I like reading when I go to bed.
... I'm often hungry when I walk.
... I don't want to be thirsty.
... I don't want to be cold at night.
... they're very comfortable.

1 I'll take a sleeping bag because I don't want to be cold at night.

2 I'll take two bottles of water because I don't want to be thirsty.

3 I'll take my e-reader because I like reading when I go to bed.

4 I'll take my mobile because my mum wants to know that I'm OK.

5 I'll take crisps because I'm often hungry when I walk.

► WB p. 63

[1] result *Ergebnis*

12 Your plans for the week

Imagine: you have a week's holiday.
Look at the weather forecast and think about what you'll do.

These ideas can help you to write your sentences:

On ... it'll be	hot, sunny, rainy, snowy, windy,	so I'll probably so I'll maybe so I think I'll	go play invite ...	surfing / hang gliding / shopping; for a trip in my sports car / in my private helicopter; to the beach / a restaurant with ...; football / cards with ...; some friends to my house ...

▸ WB p. 65

Unit 6

8 Choosing a topic for a poster.

17

a) Listen to the conversation and draw lines.

You don't need all the answers.

Why?
more exciting
easier
amazing
has magic and legends
interesting

Topics
The Romans in Britain
Smugglers on Britain's south coast
The Pilgrims
King Arthur

Why not?
really boring
not favourite topic
did that in history
too difficult
don't have enough information

- Which topic do they choose? King Arthur

▸ WB p. 78

Unit 1

1 What they did in the holidays

1 *swimming* 2 *summer camp* 3 *lake*
4 *family barbecue* 5 *mountains* 6 *Spain*

2 Luca's brother Jack sees his friend Wayne

Jack ____ Hi Wayne. *Nice* to *see* you again.

Wayne _ *Hi* Jack. *Give* me *five*! How *were your* holidays?

Jack ____ They were OK, *thanks*. I *stayed* in bed *late* every day. *What about* you?

Wayne _ I *went* to Turkey *with* my family in *August*. It *was* fun!

Jack ____ What was the *weather* like?

Wayne _ *It was* hot and *sunny*. I didn't *want* to come *home*!

3 Ellie's friend John talks about the holidays.

In the holidays I *went* to Scotland and *stayed* with my uncle in St Andrews. It *was* great! I *didn't know* St Andrews before – I really *liked* the town and I *loved* the beach. My uncle *bought* a ball and we *played* football on the beach every day. We *had* lots of barbecues in the garden. I *didn't miss* my friends – and I *made* a new friend – my uncle's new dog! I *didn't want* to come home!

4 School clubs

Emily ____ I'd like to *join the homework club.*

Seb ____ *I'd like to join the music club.*

Caroline _ *I'd like to join the science club.*

Evan ____ I'd like to *join the karate club.*

Julia ____ I'd like to *join the book club.*

Jason ____ I'd like to join the *cooking club.*

5 John's dream

1 *Wrong* 2 *Right* 3 *Not in the text* 4 *Wrong*
5 *Right* 6 *Wrong* 7 *Not in the text*

Unit 2

1 A guy for Guy Hawkes day

shirt *trousers* *hat* *mask* *pullover* *jacket* *trainers*

2 John asks for directions

a) 1 *way* 2 *along* 3 *cross* 4 *on* 5 *lights* 6 *here*
7 *turn* 8 *much* 9 *past* 10 *near* 11 *excuse*

b) He buys *sweets*.

3 Last Sunday

1 When did *you get up on Sunday*?
2 *What did you do in the morning*?
3 *Where did you have lunch?*

4 A singer's Saturday

On Saturday morning I usually go to the gym, but last Saturday I *didn't go* there because I had a concert in the evening. I *had* lunch at a top restaurant with my friends, but I *didn't drink* any alcohol because I *wanted* to be at my best for the concert. I *didn't do* anything in the afternoon – I just *stayed* at home and *listened* to music (but I *didn't listen* to my own music!). In the evening I *went* to the theatre for the concert. Usually, I feel very nervous, but this time I only *felt* a bit nervous – then I *saw* the audience! There were thousands of fans! I *sang* really well and the concert *was* great – the fans *didn't want* it to finish! I *had* a really great time. I usually get up at about 8am, but on Sunday I was really tired so I *didn't get up* early. I *stayed* in bed all morning and *got up* at lunchtime.

Unit 3

1 An alphabet of sports and hobbies

Abseiling, *badminton*, *chilling*, *darts*, extreme ironing, *football*, *games*, *hockey*, *ice skating*, *jogging*, karting, line *dancing*, *meeting* friends, *netball*, *outdoor sports*, *pop concerts*, quizzes, *rugby*, *swimming*, *taking photos*, underwater swimming, *volleyball*, *watching TV*, xylophone, yachting, *zoo* visits.

2 TV in Germany

1 The best music show is ...
2 The most *exciting crime series is ...*
3 *The funniest comedy show is ...*
4 *The most popular soap is ...*
5 *The most boring programme is ...*
6 *The best reality show is ...*
7 *The most interesting documentary is ...*
8 *The worst TV programme is ...*

3 In your town or village

Examples: This is the school where I went when I was small. Those are the oldest houses in our village. That's the bus stop where I get the bus every morning. These are the best pizzas in town!

4 An interview about chores

Examples: Do you hoover the house? Do you fill the dishwasher? Do you tidy your room? Do you cut the grass? Do you wash up?

5 A scary hobby

1 He does ghost tours.
2 He does them in the evenings in summer.
3 He started when he was 17.
4 They are scary, but funny too.
5 I (wouldn't like this hobby because I don't like scary stories!)

---

10 Animal quiz: answers

1 c (850 km) 2 b (cheetah) 3 c (koala) 4 a (10 cm) 5 a (blue whale) 6 c (mosquito)

Unit 4

1 Your food pyramid

b) *Examples:* 1 I drink lots of water. 2 I eat too many potatoes.
3 I don't eat enough vegetables.

2 At the doctor's

a) Mrs Graves: Picture 5 Mr Robertson: Picture 4 Miss Abbot: Picture 1 Mr Jones: Picture 3

b) 1 Mrs Graves hasn't slept well for about two weeks. She's worried because her son has lost his job.
2 Mr Robertson has had his problem for two days. The doctor says he should go to the hospital.
3 The doctor tells Miss Abbot that she should be in bed. He says that she should drink lots of water or tea.
4 Mr Jones has a very sore throat. But he doesn't have a headache.

3 The Food Doctor

1 Nuts are the healthiest. 2 Dark chocolate is healthy.
3 They're good for you because you need lots of fruit.
4 They're not so healthy because they have too much sugar.

4 Maths homework

Mia ___ Oh, hi Luca. Have you *started* the maths homework yet?

Luca ___ No, I *haven't*, because Grace is here and I*'ve played* some games with her. Why, what's the matter?

Mia ___ Well, I*'ve tried* to do it, but it's too hard!

Luca ___ I'm sorry I can't help you, Mia. *Have* you *phoned* Ellie? Perhaps she's *finished* her homework.

Mia ___ No, she *hasn't*. I know because I*'ve* already *talked* to her!

5 Ellie has decided to change things

1 Ellie *has helped her mum at home.*

2 She *has eaten a good breakfast.*

3 She *has drunk lots of water.*

4 She *hasn't bought any crisps.*

5 She *has done her homework.*

6 Ellie and Zoe *haven't watched TV.*

Unit 5

1 A camping trip

a) *trainers, tent, sunglasses, boots, sleeping bag, rucksack, mobile, sun cream, map, sweets, compass, first-aid kit, whistle, plastic bag*

b) *No, they won't (go hang-gliding). They'll go climbing and mud running.*

c) *Example:*

Dear Catherine, *I'm camping with some friends on Dartmoor. The weather is good! Yesterday we went walking. It was fun because our teacher fell into the river. Today we're going hang-gliding. I think it'll be sunny tomorrow and we'll probably go climbing. I hope we won't climb very high because I don't like to look down! Best wishes …*

2 The weather forecast

a) South-west England: *rainy*; North-east England: *sunny*; Wales: *10°C*; Northern Ireland: *foggy*; Scotland: *cloudy*

b) 1 *rainy and windy, temperature – 10 degrees*

2 *no – foggy and cloudy*

3 Adjective or adverb?

1 *quickly* 2 *noisy* 3 *happily* 4 *slowly* 5 *careful* 6 *popular*

4 What do you think will happen?

1 Mark sees *a black cloud*. I think he*'ll put on his rain gear*.

2 Some people are having *a picnic*. I think they*'ll leave their litter*.

3 I think Mark *will pick up the litter* – or the ponies *will eat it*.

5 A day on Dartmoor

Example:

One Saturday afternoon Mrs Burton and her two children drove across Dartmoor. They saw some sheep on a hill. When they started to walk, it rained. They put on their boots and rain gear. When they were tired, they stopped and had a picnic. They took off their boots. After lunch they walked again. They crossed the river on an old stone bridge. Then Mrs Burton fell. She shouted because her leg hurt. Natalie phoned for help. Tim sat with his mother on the ground. When the ambulance men arrived, they asked, "What happened?" Mrs Burton told them. Mrs Burton had to go to hospital. She stayed there for four days. They were all happy when she came out.

Unit 6

1 English history

1 *their own; all over*

2 *sword; became; ruins; magician; cave*

3 *famous; attack; fought; destroyed*

4 *Protestants; sailed; ship; built*

2 What will Nils do in the holidays?

1 If I have *enough money*, I'll go *to England*.

2 If *my friend is free*, he'll *come with me*.

3 *If we're near Plymouth, we'll visit Tintagel Castle.*

4 *If we take our tents, we'll go camping.*

3 Jake's adventure at Tintagel

1 Last weekend *Jake and his mum went by car to Tintagel. The sun was shining.*

2 *They visited the castle. Jake wasn't interested. He left his mum.*

3 *Jake went down to the sea. There were lots of rocks there. The waves were a bit scary.*

4 *Suddenly a big wave took Jakes into the sea. "Help! Help" he shouted.*

5 *And suddenly he saw Arthur and Merlin. And they helped him out of the water!*

6 *Then Jake's mum came with the police. But Arthur and Merlin weren't there.*

Den vollständigen *Language file* findest du im Schülerbuch ab S.172.

Units 1 und 2

LF 6 THE SIMPLE PAST:

▸ WB pp. 5–7

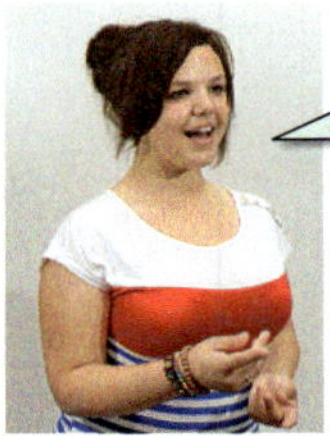

I loved the holidays. In August I went to Spain with dad. I made two new friends in the hotel. We played on the beach and we had lots of fun.

Yes, the holidays were cool. Last week I visited my cousins and yesterday I stayed in bed very late!

Mit dem ***simple past*** sagst du, was **zu einer bestimmten Zeit** in der Vergangenheit geschah. Du verwendest es oft mit Zeitangaben wie *yesterday*, *last week*, *in August*, *in 2012*. Das ***simple past*** verwendest du auch, um **Geschichten** zu erzählen.

LF 7 Positive statements

▸ WB pp. 5–6

a) Regelmäßige Verben

Die meisten Verben sind **regelmäßig**. Das ***simple past*** bildest du durch Anhängen von -***ed*** an das Verb:

Verb (Grundform)		**+ -*ed***	
stay	→	*stayed*	[-d]
ask	→	*asked*	[-t]
visit	→	*visited*	[-ɪd]

Die Vergangenheitsform ist für alle Personen gleich.

b) Unregelmäßige Verben

Unregelmäßige Verben haben ***simple past***-Formen, die du lernen musst:

Verb (Grundform)	***Simple past***
be, go, have, make	*was/were, went, had, made*

▸ *List of irregular verbs, p. 270*

Achte auf Besonderheiten bei der Schreibung: like → liked, stop → stopped, worry → worried

LF 8 Negative statements

▸ WB pp. 6–7

We didn't **go** on holiday, but last week we went to London. I helped at home too, but I didn't **help** every day.

Wenn du sagen willst, was nicht geschah, setzt du ***didn't*** vor das Verb:

– *We* ***didn't*** ***go*** *on holiday.*
– *I* ***didn't*** ***help*** *every day.*

Die Langform heißt ***did not***.

LF 9 Questions and short answers

▸ WB pp. 19–21

a) Questions

Did you **go** to the bonfire party yesterday?
Bist du gestern zur … gegangen?

Did you **wear** a costume?
Hast du ein Kostüm getragen?

Yes, I did.

No, I didn't!

Fragen im ***simple past***, die man mit „Ja" oder „Nein" beantworten kann, bildest du mit ***Did*** und der Grundform des Verbs.

Die Form ist für alle Personen gleich: immer ***Did***.

Auch bei Fragen mit Fragewort verwendest du ***did*** bei allen Personen und das Verb in der Grundform. Setze das Fragewort vor *did*:

Did *you* ***go*** *to the party yesterday?*
When did *you* ***go****?*

Bei Fragen im ***simple past*** ist das Verb in der Grundform. Aber bei den Antworten musst du das Verb in die Vergangenheitsform setzen.

What did you watch?
Was hast du dir angesehen?
When did it finish?
Wann war es zu Ende?
And where did you go then?
Und wohin bist du dann gegangen?

b) Short answers

Kurzantworten bildest du
– nach *Yes* mit *did*:
  Yes, I did. / Yes, he did. usw.
– nach *No* mit *didn't*:
  No, I didn't. / No, he didn't. usw.

Unit 3

LF 12 The comparison of adjectives

▸ *WB pp. 33–34*

1 Bei kurzen (einsilbigen) Adjektiven und bei Adjektiven mit der Endung ***-y*** hängst du für die Steigerung *-er* und *-est* an das Adjektiv:

Cyril is cool.
Sandy thinks she's cooler than Cyril.
But Babe thinks he's the coolest.

Beachte die Besonderheiten der Schreibweise:

nice	*nicer*	*(the) nicest*
*friendl**y***	*friendlier*	*(the) friendliest*
big	*bigger*	*(the) biggest*

2 Bei längeren (zwei- oder dreisilbigen) Adjektiven stellst du ***more*** und ***most*** vor das Adjektiv:

popular	*more popular*	*(the) most popular*
boring	*more boring*	*(the) most boring*

Babe thinks he's the most popular crab, but Cyril says he's the most boring.

3 Einige Adjektive werden unregelmäßig gesteigert. Die Formen musst du auswendig lernen, z.B.

good	*better*	*(the) best*
much / many	*more*	*(the) most*

Unit 4

LF 14 The present perfect

▸ *WB pp. 50–51*

Mit dem ***present perfect*** drückst du aus, dass etwas **irgendwann bereits** (oder noch nie) geschehen ist. Es ist unwichtig, wann es geschehen ist. Deshalb wird auch kein genauer Zeitpunkt angegeben.

Oft hat die Handlung **Auswirkungen** auf die Gegenwart oder Zukunft:

... and he has drunk my water. So I'm thirsty too.
Buster hat Adams Wasser getrunken.
Ergebnis: Jetzt hat Adam Durst.

Du bildest das ***present perfect*** mit:

have / has + **3. Form des Verbs**
('ve / 's) ***(past participle)***

Bildung des ***past participle***:

Bei **regelmäßigen** Verben hängst du ***-ed*** an die Grundform an (wie beim *simple past*):
happen → happened, finish → finished

Two bad things *have* just *happened*, Luca.
I'm hungry because Buster *has eaten* my ice cream – and he *has drunk* my water.
So I'm thirsty too.

Oh, Buster! What *have* you *done*? *Have* you really *eaten* Adam's ice cream? Yes, you *have*!

Well, I'*ve* already *finished* my sandwiches, Adam, but I *haven't eaten* my apple yet. So here you are.

Unregelmäßige Verben haben besondere Formen, die du lernen musst:

Grundform *(infinitive)*	***simple past***	***past participle***
eat	*ate*	*eaten*
drink	*drank*	*drunk*

▸ *List of irregular verbs, p. 270*

Unit 5

LF 16 The *will*-future

▸ *WB pp. 64–65*

I think everybody *will* **like** our trip.
I'm sure it *won't* **be** boring.
Will it **rain**?

No, it *won't*. It *will* **be** sunny and a bit foggy.
We*'ll* **have** a great time.
You*'ll* **see**.

Merke:
Das Englische *I will* heißt im Deutschen „ich werde" und nicht „ich will":

I will	➔	ich werde
I want to	➔	ich will / möchte

Mit dem ***will-future*** kannst du über die Zukunft sprechen, z.B. **Vermutungen** und **Vorhersagen** äußern.

Eine **Vermutung** fängt oft an mit: *I think* (ich denke / glaube), *I'm sure* (ich bin sicher) oder *maybe* (vielleicht).
– *I think everybody will like our trip.*
Ich denke, alle werden unseren Ausflug mögen.

Bei **Vorhersagen** geht es oft um Dinge, die man nicht beeinflussen kann, z.B. das Wetter.
– *It won't rain.* Es wird nicht regnen.

Mit dem ***will-future*** kannst du einen spontanen Entschluss, z. B. ein Hilfsangebot, äußern:
Don't move. We'll help you, said Mia.

Du bildest das ***will-future*** mit ***will*** **+ Verb** (Grundform)

Die Kurzform von *will* heißt *'ll*.
Die Verneinung heißt *will not* (Kurzform *won't*).
Die Frage bildest du mit *will* oder *won't* + I/you/he/...
– *Will I be happy? Won't she be angry?*
Die Kurzantworten heißen: *Yes, I will*/*No, I won't* usw.

Die Formen *will* und *won't* sind für alle Personen gleich.

Unit 6

LF 18 The past progressive

▸ *WB p. 79*

Mit dem ***past progressive*** drückst du aus, dass eine (meist längere) Handlung in der Vergangenheit **gerade im Gange** war:
– *The friends were visiting an old castle.*
Die Freunde waren gerade dabei, eine alte Burg zu besuchen.

Mit dem ***past progressive*** beschreibst du auch, was gerade vor sich ging, als etwas anderes geschah *(simple past)*:
– *The friends were walking through the halls when suddenly they heard a drum.*
Die Freunde gingen (gerade) durch die Hallen, als sie plötzlich eine Trommel hörten.

Das ***past progressive*** bildest du mit
was / were + verb + -ing:
I / He / She / It was playing a drum.
We / You / They were playing a drum.

QUELLENVERZEICHNIS

Illustrationen

Kate Davies, Colerne (S.3; S.5; S.15; S.16; S.21; S.30; S.31; S.42 unten; S.48; S.53; S.55; S.57; S.58; S.62 oben; S.64; S.66; S.68; S.71; S.73; S.74; S.81; S.82); **Katrin Inzinger**, Berlin (S.2; S.7; S.13; S.26; S.28; S.33; S.36; S.42 oben; S.43 oben; S.45; S.46; S.47; S.50; S.65; S.72; S.75; S.83; S.84); **Jeongsook Lee**, Heidelberg (S.62 unten)

Bildquellen

Alamy, Abingdon (S.6 / Andy Lane; S.23 / patrick nairne; S.25 Science Museum / David Pearson; S.54 Radius Images; S.60 pony / Penny Tweedie; S.61.7 trousers / Jason Batterham, 1 / Martin Shields; S.67 Blickwinkel; S.69 / ableimages); **Trevor Burrows Photography**, Plymouth (S.17 unten; S.58); **Fotolia**, Berlin (S.44 biking / Jacek Chabraszewski; S.61.7 jacket / beauty of life); **Istockphoto**, Calgary (S.68 / Aimstock); **Shutterstock**, New York (S.10 / c.byatt-norman; S.11 / Stephen Rees; S.17 cat / Tony Campbell; S.18 / Erik Lam; S.25 Big Ben / nevenm, London Eye / Keattikorn, Tower Bridge / Andrew Barker, Buckingham Palace / Renata Sedmakova, Hyde Park / zhangyouyang; S.32 grey hoodie / sagir, Striped hoodie / sagir, walking boots / forest badger, wellies / mojito.mak[dog]gmail[dot]com, yellow cap / windu, cap / Elif Eren, sunglasses / Elnur, heart sunglasses / 3D Stock; S.34 mobile / bloomua, phone / Madarakis, book / LanKS, Ereader / bloomua, cat / Eric Isselee, dog/ MilsiArt, geography / Pressmaster , maths / Tomasz Trojanowski , small dog / cynoclub; S.41 badminton / terekhov igor, darts / Julian Rovagnati, games / Filip Fuxa, hockey / Rob Byron, jogging / Warren Goldswain, line dancing / Lorraine Swanson, rugby / Lorelyn Medina, camera / Julia Ivantsova; S.43 dog / WilleeCole; S.44 lake / ASchindl, mountains / Fedor Selivanov; S.49.1 / Jacek Chabraszewski, 2 / Liz Van Steenburgh, 3 / Stuart Monk, 4 / Gordana Sermek, 5 / Olga Ekaterincheva, 6 / Iakov Filimonov; S.53 / Paul Brennan; S.65 thermometer / Milena Vuckovic; S.71 oben / Haver; S.72 map / Ashley van Dyck, weather icons/ ronfromyork; S.79.1 / Yarek Gora, 2 / StockLite, 3 / Max Topchii, 4 / Kamira, 5 / Mandy Godbehear, 6 / Gravicapa)

Titelbild

Trevor Burrows Photography, Plymouth